$\mathscr{A}$ KANSAS SOLDIER AT WAR

A KANSAS SOLDIER AT WAR

THE CIVIL WAR LETTERS OF
CHRISTIAN & ELISE DUBACH ISELY

KEN SPURGEON

Charleston   London

THE
History
PRESS

Published by The History Press
Charleston, SC 29403
www.historypress.net

Cover images: *Front*: C.H. Isely sketch (background) courtesy of Wichita State University Libraries; images of Christian and Elise courtesy of the Isely family. *Back*: Flag drawing courtesy of the Kansas State Historical Society; image of the Iselys courtesy of the Isely family.

First published 2013

Manufactured in the United States

ISBN 978.1.62619.015.3

Library of Congress CIP data applied for.

Notice: The information in this book is true and complete to the best of our knowledge. It is offered without guarantee on the part of the author or The History Press. The author and The History Press disclaim all liability in connection with the use of this book.

Lovingly dedicated to the memory of

servants of God and guardians of the republic

Lawrence J. Murray (1927–2001),

Robert J. Martin (1916–1994)

and

Joseph M. Spurgeon (1842–1877), 9ᵗʰ Kansas Cavalry, Company E,

a fellow Kansas soldier

There are persons who would snear [sic] *at, and condemn my sentiments; but I thank God, although such would uphold slavery and fetter the mind, <u>I am not their slave yet</u>. I do not want their favors. I care not for their frowns, but will do my duty to my God and my country, regardless of their secret midnight meetings, their conspirings against us, to contemplate our overthrow. Of my work I am not ashamed, nor afraid to do it in open daylight, because it is the work of humanity, justice and right.*

O my poor bleeding and distracted Land, many and various are thine ungrateful enemies; but to me thou art dearest of all others; should my friends forsake and betray thee, yet never could I cease to love thee. For thee, and the flag of thy braves I have shed many burning tears, and offered my fervent prayers to God; for thee I forsook my sweet home and darling friends, and now sacrificed my health without a murmur; and if necessary will yet lay down my humble life, and take my last resting place on one of Arkansas' rocky hills beneath the branches of a lonely oak or pine tree, far from home and loved ones, unnoticed and unwept for—<u>only may I never see the Sun of thy Glory go down, nor thy beautiful Union severed</u>.

Christian H. Isely
September 24, 1864

CONTENTS

PREFACE

Christian and Elise Dubach Isely were Swiss immigrants who came to America in 1831 and 1854, respectively. They were married in May 1861 and resided in St. Joseph, Missouri, where they found themselves in the midst of the American Civil War. During the next three years, as they were separated by the conflict, they wrote hundreds of letters to each other, as well as to other friends and family members. In the case of Christian, he kept a diary for much of the war. These letters and diary entries compose the bulk of what was used in this study. The majority of these letters are in the Isely Family Papers at the Wichita State University's Special Collections, Ablah Library. Also consulted were a few Isely items located in various collections at the Kansas State Historical Society.

Another primary source is the collection Isely Family Correspondence and Miscellaneous Documents, 1849–1943, part of the Kansas Collection at the Spencer Research Library, University of Kansas. This collection has many prewar letters in addition to some written in German. A few of these letters were translated by a student, Annemarie Ostrowski, in a paper she wrote some years ago in an American studies class for Professor Norman Yetman. Additional letters and diary entries belonging to private collections were typed by David McGuire and included in *Uncommon Writings by Common Folk: The Isely Family Letters, Papers, and Diaries* (1988). Another significant source that was extremely insightful is Elise's autobiography, *Sunbonnet Days*, written in 1935.

Regimental histories produced by the adjutant general of the State of Kansas were quite helpful, as were communications by members of the 2nd

Kansas Cavalry, located in the *Official Records of the War of the Rebellion*. Many secondary histories of both the Kansas-Missouri conflict and the war in general were of great benefit and are listed in the bibliography. The result of this research produced a unique story because the Iselys expressed both the military and civilian perspectives of a part of the war (from 1861 to 1864) for which primary accounts are less common. The result is a passionate exchange between husband and wife in which the border war and its causes are discussed openly and frankly.

ACKNOWLEDGEMENTS

No amount of words, however carefully crafted, could ever express my debt of gratitude for aid and support with this work. First, I express special thanks to my wife, Amy, to our four children—Lauren, Rebecca, Sarah and Jonathan—and to my son-in-law, Brandon Pope. My parents, R.L. and Donna Spurgeon, have always given me unconditional love and understanding, and they have also selflessly given me their ears when I am sure the subject was less than interesting to them. My siblings and extended family and my in-laws, Leon and Judy Embry, have always been supportive and kind, for which I'm very grateful. Several of my own relatives were people of strong faith and patriotism, and often when I read a letter or a diary entry, my mind reflected on those loved ones. I am also very thankful for the support of my school, Northfield School of the Liberal Arts, and its leadership, Philip and Becky Elder and Jim Graf, who have always listened and been very encouraging.

I give special mention to the tremendous encouragement that I received from my advisors and teachers. So many could be acknowledged, but a few have given me particular attention, for which I am grateful. This work was initially my master's thesis, and so thanks certainly are due to several graduate advisors. I first extend special thanks to Dr. Will Klunder, who as my thesis chair helped to shape the work and was very helpful in giving me focus. Next, I express thanks to the late Dr. John Born, longtime early American historian at Wichita State University, who twenty years ago cultivated in me a love for American history. His passion for the subject is the reason that I, too, wanted to be a historian. It was Dr. Born who, after my absence from college, clasped my hand and told me that I should be back in school and that one day I would be a history teacher, inspiring young people. I will never forget that encounter. It was far more inspirational to me than he ever knew. Next, the late Dr. Craig Miner taught me valuable lessons and showed true enthusiasm for his subject, and this was a great motivator to me in my endeavors. He was, in my opinion, the greatest historian of Kansas, and I was blessed to study under him and later become his friend. Mike Kelly, the former curator of Special Collections at Wichita State University, and Mary Nelson, program consultant of Special Collections, were always available to me. Both Mike and Mary were happy to see someone taking such interest in the Isely Collection, and they gave me excellent advice and encouragement in completing this project. Other members of the faculty at Wichita State University were also helpful. So many of them took the time to inquire of my progression and offered kind words of encouragement. Lastly, I give thanks to Mrs. Helen Miller, my sixth-grade teacher at South Hillside Elementary. Mrs. Miller, like Dr. Born, could never have known what an inspiration her enthusiasm about history provided me. She, along with family members, taught me that history is not an accumulation of dusty, dead words but the reflection of people who lived, loved and made difficult decisions.

I owe a special and heartfelt thanks to the Isely family. Peggi Bell Johnson and David McGuire and the late Katherine McGuire were kind enough to have me spend two memorable days in January 2000 at their home. Katherine was the granddaughter of Christian and Elise, and she, along with a grandson, the late Kenny Isely, provided me with interesting insights about their grandparents. I soon found out that David McGuire, Katherine's husband, was an integral part of the Isely story. In the 1980s and 1990s, David endeavored to gather much of what would become the Isely Collection. After getting a handle on what existed, David painstakingly read and typed the contents of the bulk of these letters and diaries. His typed letters gave me a great advantage. Being able to talk to him about the collection also aided me because he had looked at the collection so closely. Great-granddaughter Peggi Bell Johnson has been kind enough to keep in contact with me for several years. When I had a question or need, she has been very helpful in trying to address it. Other family members, including Karl Isely and John Mattox, were also very supportive and generous to me.

As I prepared the book for publication, others have come to my aid, for which I am appreciative. Thanks to Bill Coleman and Donna Payne Hughes for editorial assistance and feedback and to my sister, Bev Shafer, for commentary and feedback. Thanks to my friend Matt Walker for photograph and art assistance, as well as for the maps. Thanks to Blair Tarr and Nancy Sherbert at the Kansas State Historical Society. Thanks to Jim Spencer for his advice and counsel. Thanks to my many reenacting and fellow historian pards over the years in the 8th Kansas Volunteer Infantry, USA; the 9th Texas, CSA; and the Sons of Union Veterans, Department of Kansas.

Like the Iselys, I concur that in everything, which includes this work, the utmost thanks goes to the Lord. Like Christian, I believe that my duty is first to God. I'm thankful for my many Christian mentors through the years and for wonderful pastors. Also like the Iselys, I am thankful for the preservation of the Union. I thank God that so many have given so much to preserve and protect this nation because they cherished so highly the concepts set forth by our founders. We have all been blessed by their sacrifices and selflessness.

Last but not least, I must thank Christian and Elise Dubach Isely. Although they have long since departed, it was their wonderfully descriptive and passionate letters that made my interest soar when I first read them in 1992. I could not believe that this story had not been told. To me, it was of tremendous interest on several fronts. In all of our lives, through word and deed, we demonstrate what our lives are truly about. For Christian and Elise, as the collection demonstrates, they lived for God and country.

CHAPTER 1
COMING TO AMERICA

The American Civil War began in April 1861. The thought of armed conflict came as a shock to many. It was not, however, a surprise to those who inhabited the area of the Kansas-Missouri border. For them, the war was merely a continuation of a seven-year feud over the extension of slavery. The Kansas-Missouri border situation in the 1850s, or "Bleeding Kansas" as it came to be known, was in many ways a microcosm of the Civil War and its causes. The participants were common people thrust into an uncommon situation. Two such individuals, Christian and Elise Dubach Isely, found themselves at the heart of the conflict in the late 1850s and early 1860s.

The history of most Americans is a story of immigrants. They came for a variety of reasons, but all thought, or hoped, for a better life in a new country far away from Old World aristocracy. They sought a new world with less entrenched prejudices and with more opportunity for success. Unfortunately, many found an imperfect new world, not the utopia they hoped for. Still, they came, all looking for something new, different and unique. Once here, most never returned. They were now Americans, and they had to decide to embrace this new land, its ways and at least a portion of its culture or live as outsiders in this new land of opportunity.

Such was the case with the families of Christian and Margaret Elizabeth "Eliza" Dubach Isely, immigrants whose families came at different times, trying to seize the promise and opportunity of the American dream. Christian was born on May 3, 1828, in Oberthal, Canton Berne, Switzerland, the son of Christian and Barbara Ozenberger Isely. The family immigrated to the

United States in 1831. The journey began in a covered wagon heading to Havre, France. The family then boarded a sailing vessel for New York City. After traveling by steamboat to Albany and then Cleveland, the Isely family bought horses and drove them to Holmes County in central Ohio, arriving in the fall of 1831. The family, all German speakers, attended Reformed Church parochial schools, where the lessons were conducted wholly in German. After making a tearful plea to his father, Christian was allowed to attend English-speaking public schools for six months.

In 1850, the twenty-two-year-old Christian, probably out of a sense of adventure, migrated to St. Joseph, Missouri, by steamboat. He worked at a variety of vocations and places during the next three years, including rafting logs to St. Louis, laboring in Wisconsin lumber camps and, finally, working as a carpenter in St. Joseph. In 1854, with the organization of the Kansas-Nebraska territories, Christian (or "C.H.," as he was sometimes called) led a group of Swiss immigrants into Nebraska. They settled in Richardson County, in southeast Nebraska, where a creek still bears the name Easily (for Isely) at the spot where Christian established his claim. The other colonists had little interest in learning to speak the English language of their new homeland, however, and an apparently angered Christian relinquished his claim in the mid-1850s and resumed life as a carpenter in the burgeoning town of St. Joseph, Missouri.[1]

Elise Dubach Isely was born on June 21, 1842, in Courrendlin, Canton Berne, Switzerland.[2] She grew up primarily on a dairy farm in Mount Orvin in Switzerland, the eldest of three children born to Benjamin and Jeanette Dubach. Elise was followed by a brother, Adolph, two years her junior, and Fred, who was four years younger.

Elise's childhood was spent in the shadows of the beautiful Swiss Alps. She was exposed at a young age to a variety of language and dialects. Her father was a German speaker and always addressed the children in that language. Her mother, Jeanette, was a native of France. The children were encouraged to talk to their mother in French and their father in German. In addition to this, Elise spoke the vernacular of the region, Swiss patois. Elise attended public schools that conducted their lessons in French.

Elise remembered many years later that her parents received a thrilling letter in 1854. The letter, sent from St. Joseph, Missouri, by Elise's uncle, Christian Dubach, encouraged the family to come to the United States as soon as possible. Elise's uncle claimed that if "you remain in Switzerland, you will grow old without being any better off than you are today." Christian Dubach told of how land in America was plentiful and that a tremendous opportunity existed with the passage of the Kansas-Nebraska Act: "So generous are the Americans that they have even given the right to foreigners to vote in these two territories within six months after they have made their declaration of becoming citizens in the United States."

Elise recalled that her family never thought of themselves as poor until her uncle's letter arrived from America. Elise's father read the letter over and over. One part amazed him tremendously. Uncle Christian stated that they needed to sell the better part of their clothing before sailing to America. "In America," he wrote, "the people launder every Monday; therefore, you will need few changes." This dumbfounded Elise. How could these people launder every week? In Switzerland, they laundered twice a year. Clothes were washed in the autumn and in the spring. Washing clothes was a major endeavor that required everyone's help. Many people owned up to fifty changes of clothes. Elise had no idea how much her life was about to change.

Leaving their Swiss home was to be a great adventure, but Elise soon realized that leaving also meant saying goodbye to dear friends. All the talk at Elise's school centered on the upcoming voyage: "The teacher showed her interest by uncovering a wall chart and hunting out on the map such places as New Orleans and the Mississippi and Missouri rivers." The stir at school was nothing compared to the preparations being made at home. Elise's mother, Jeanette, rendered butter in a kettle on the stove: "She boiled the butter until it became clear, then poured it into buckets where it cooled and hardened again." Twelve buckets in all were prepared for the voyage. As steerage passengers, the Dubachs had to sustain themselves on the cheeses, dried prunes, dried cherries and dried apples they had packed. Elise's father, Benjamin, provided two large wooden sea chests and a large trunk. "Everything else had to be disposed of. Part of our surplus clothing we donated to the poor." The rest of the family's clothing was sold at auction. Elise later recalled that her father had given away many of his linen shirts but still sold thirty-six at auction and that her mother sold sixty pieces of fine homespun linen underclothes.

Before departing, Elise's girlfriends "held a coasting party in my honor." For hours, the girls with their hand sleds coasted down the slopes of Orvin. Most had a wonderful time, but Elise's best friend, Louise Schmidt, "rained tears all over a hand-knit purse she gave me." Elise related that had Louise's parents been willing, she would have joined the Dubach family on their trip to America. Finally, the day came in early February. "We left the mountainside buried under huge drifts of snow," Elise wrote in her diary. "The next spring mountain flowers would bloom beside the melting snowbanks, but one Swiss girl and her two Swiss brothers would not be there to gather the Edelweiss nor to play with the goats and calves as they came out to crop the first blades of grass."

Traveling first by wagon and train, the family arrived at Havre, France, where they boarded the *Searampore*, an English three-masted vessel. Since the crew was composed of Englishmen, the Dubachs could not understand their language. Still, Elise related that through "loud yells and menacing looks" it was made apparent what they needed to do. For twelve-year-old Elise, the crew was "hard-looking." Some of the crew boasted that they had been pirates, "a thing we could well believe from the evil glances of their eyes and from the red scars of knife wounds decorating their faces." Elise was amazed at much on her voyage, but the manner in which the various passengers cooked their meals was the first surprise. The seamen would shout that it was time to come on deck to cook. Eight sheds, called kitchens, were assigned to the steerage: "Under each roof was a long iron rod from which the kettles could be suspended. Fire was laid by the seamen in the troughs; and when the billets of wood were burned to red hot coals, the passengers were summoned to cook." Those who did not respond immediately were simply out of luck; there would be no more fire until the next meal. Water was rationed as well, so anyone spilling water from the kettle could get no more until the next meal.

Another event that grabbed Elise's attention upon departure was the plight of a woman who began screaming upon the ship's move from port. She was crying in German that she had boarded and was being carried away by mistake. Her son followed, explaining to her that he had decoyed her on board. Elise learned that the woman's husband and daughter had come to America the previous year, but when it came time for the mother to follow her husband across the ocean, she had lost heart. "Those were perilous times to go to sea, for many a ship left port never to return," said Elise. The woman had thought that she was on board to aid her son in departing. He had purposely detained her below deck. Elise reported that the woman remained on the ship and that both mother and son made it safely to America.

As the voyage began in earnest, Elise realized that theft and hardship were a part of life. With four hundred passengers on board, word of any event became public knowledge and was shared among the passengers. While most of the news was trivial in nature, occasionally something very important was passed along from berth to berth. While Elise mentioned that every precaution was made to keep the ship sanitary, people fell ill from time to time, and some passengers had boarded ill. It was reported that a two-year-old German girl was very sick. "Curious strangers crowded about her berth," Elise recalled, "when she expired, the news was quickly relayed from one passenger to another till everybody knew it." The captain assigned two sailors with a sheet of sail cloth, long darning needles and stout white cord to wrap the body and sew it firmly from head to foot. A weight was tied to the feet. The body was stretched out on a board to be lowered "reverently over the side by the two sailors." A priest who was a passenger read a burial service. As the sailor at the foot of the board let out six feet of rope, the body slid into the water. Elise remembered, "The iron weight instantly carried it out of sight into the deep. The sailors comforted the parents with the assurance that the weight would haul the body so far beneath the surface that the sharks would never find it."[3]

Following a storm and harshly imposed restrictions on water and provisions, the voyage by late March reached the Florida Straits, bound for New Orleans. One night, as Elise went to bed, the passengers were told that in the morning they would be able to see the American shore. Elise was so excited that she couldn't sleep for some time. She finally did doze off, only to awaken to the lookout shouting, "Land, Land!" Elise recalled, "The cry was followed by a wild song and dance by the sailors.... Looking over the rail, I saw for the first time the hazy outline of the low-lying Louisiana coast." A tugboat came out and was soon lugging the *Serampore* into the river channel.

As people began to depart, Elise looked down and saw the heinous individual whom the passengers had despised throughout the voyage standing on the levee, "ogling at the women." The passengers had referred to this ex-pirate with crooked eyes as "*Rot Teufel*," which meant red devil. Elise reported that throughout the entire voyage he had yelled at the children, abused the men and insulted the women. It was nothing to see him slapping or kicking any person who got in his way. Now, as the passengers were unloading, the "*Rot Teufel*" was at it again with a new group of unsuspecting immigrants. At sea, the passengers had to endure this man, as to fight him could have resulted in mutiny. On land, things were different. Elise said that her father was a mild man but that as soon his feet touched the levee, he jumped toward the redheaded pirate. Benjamin Dubach dealt the pirate with a blow on the chin that felled him. "At the same instant several other men also struck him; then two or three score women, each of whom had suffered all sorts of indignities aboard ship, rushed him," recalled Elise. The women proceeded to pull the pirate's hair, yank his ears and twist his nose. "Loudly did *Rot Teufel* bawl for help," wrote Elise, "but before any of his sailor friends could fight their way to his side, the women resumed their business."[4]

The Dubachs and their belongings were on the American shore. They had arrived after a sea voyage of fifty-six days. It was April 9, 1855.

The voyage to America was complete, but not the voyage to the Dubachs' destination of St. Joseph. At New Orleans, Benjamin Dubach proceeded to the office of a steamboat company and purchased tickets to sail for St. Louis in two days. The family then spent those days rambling through the old French quarter of New Orleans. The French signs and language were an encouragement to the Dubachs, who could converse with French speakers and comprehend the signs and conversation around them. Finally, the steamboat, a passenger ship and a freight liner headed north up the Mississippi River. The trip took nearly two weeks as the boat stopped several times along the river.

Once they reached St. Louis, the family had to change ships again as they headed west for St. Joseph. Elise liked the Missouri River better than the lower Mississippi: "The Missouri passes through a beautiful country with ever varying scenery. Lovely cliffs and bluffs line the bottom lands or come right down to the channel. At every break in the bluffs we saw farm lands and farm buildings pass in an ever-changing vista." To Elise, the skill of the pilots was evidenced in their navigation of various danger points along the river: "Every day I had occasion to hold my breath as the man at the wheel skillfully tempted the perils of that untamed river." Half-floating trees, shifting sandbars and overhanging cliffs made navigation a constant adventure. Elise wrote that "the highest paid pilot was he who could take the boat near enough to the cliffs to avoid sandbars, yet far enough away to avoid being caught should the bank cave in." Elise had no recollection of any of the harbor towns on the Missouri because at that time none of these communities was of notable size. "Even Kansas City was then a mere village of five hundred people living along a dirt street…to us it was merely another landing, and I have no recollection of seeing it at all." In later years, Elise remembered that no one contemplated or imagined that Kansas City would ever be as important as St. Joseph.[5]

Finally, on May 6, 1855, the river journey came to an end. Word was passed that just "beyond a crook in the river was the goal of our three months' journey. With eyes turned toward the bend, each passenger was eager to catch the first view of the metropolis." Suddenly, a passenger pointed and shouted, "There she is!" First the church spires appeared. Then, as they rounded the bluff, the city lay "along the water front and pushing back between the Blacksnake Hills." People crowded the levees as the steamboat neared the dock, clanging its bell continuously. "We scanned the sea of faces along the levee. Strange faces they were of an alien people among whom we were to make our home." The men wore cowhide boots, Elise remembered, and slouch hats, but "here and there was a silk-hatted merchant." Suddenly Elise's mother, Jeanette, pointed at a face on the levee. "There's Uncle Christian!" she cried. Christian waved back, and as they came off the ship, their uncle led them to his boardinghouse, where he introduced them to their Aunt Christine, who welcomed the Dubachs to their new home.

The joy of the family in their new home was to be short-lived. Two weeks after arriving in St. Joseph, Elise's mother, Jeanette, who had been well throughout the voyage, fell ill and died. Elise wrote that it was good that she had given her doll to Elise Jendervin before their voyage to America, "for in the same grave with my mother I buried my childhood." Although she was one month short of thirteen years old, Elise no longer had time for dolls: "I had to be mother to my two younger brothers and soon was to be housekeeper for my father."[6]

Chapter 2
BLEEDING KANSAS

The death of Jeanette Dubach not only shocked the Dubachs but also left Benjamin as a single parent who needed to provide quickly for his young family. He had no interest in working in the city of St. Joseph or helping his brother, Christian Dubach, run his boardinghouse. Instead, Benjamin Dubach's thoughts were on the new lands open to settlement in the Kansas territory. Like so many others, he eagerly obtained a claim. With the lateness of the planting season, however, Benjamin had to wait until the next year to plant crops and make a go of farming his new land. In the meantime, Uncle Christian advised his brother to stay the year at his boardinghouse. When the school year started, Benjamin encouraged Elise to attend and begin to learn English. She was enrolled in a convent for a short time and slowly began to embrace her new country and language.[7]

The Kansas-Nebraska Act provided great possibilities to many new immigrants hungry for opportunity, including Benjamin Dubach. Most of these immigrants, coming from foreign lands, understood little of the political and sectional differences embroiling the nation in a conflict over slavery extension. When the Kansas-Nebraska bill was introduced in early 1854 by Senator Stephen A. Douglas of Illinois, few had any idea of the firestorm that it would create. Douglas's proposal left the decision of slavery to "the people residing therein, through their appropriate representatives," a concept referred to as "popular sovereignty." To ensure passage of his bill, Douglas was compelled to add an amendment that explicitly repealed the Missouri Compromise line that prohibited slavery north of 36°, 30'.[8]

The final version of Douglas's bill separated the territory into two: Kansas, immediately to the west of Missouri, and Nebraska, to the north of Kansas and to the west of Iowa. Many Americans assumed that Kansas was to be a slave state and Nebraska a free state. Douglas, who had larger aspirations for public office as well as a dream to move Americans west, felt the need to placate both north and south. To southerners, his repeal of the compromise gave them a chance at a slave territory in the West if they moved quickly to settle and establish their way of life. He allayed the fears of northerners by arguing that nature would prevent slavery from gaining a foothold in the new territory because the climate and landscape of Kansas were different from Missouri and other slave states. That was not totally true. In fact, much of eastern Kansas was very much like Missouri and could be used to grow hemp and tobacco. Douglas's attempts to placate both sides eventually fell flat.

The passage of the Kansas-Nebraska bill set off an unbelievable fervor. Northerners and southerners began to do everything in their power to encourage large groups to migrate to the territories, especially to Kansas. One St. Louis newspaper argued that if the region became free, "Missouri will be surrounded on three sides by free territory, where there will always be men and means to assist in the escape of our slaves…. This species of property would become insecure if not valueless in Missouri." Missouri senator David Atchison fervently pledged "to extend the institutions of Missouri over the Territory to whatever sacrifice of blood or treasure." Atchison, who was the president pro tempore of the Senate, added that he would see the region "sink in hell" before it became a free territory. *New York Tribune* newspaper editor Horace Greeley calculated that "the bill created more abolitionists in two months than William Lloyd Garrison and Wendell Phillips had created in twenty years." New York senator William H. Seward bluntly warned, "Come on then, gentleman of the slave states, since there is no escaping your challenge, I accept it, in behalf of freedom. We will engage in a competition for the virgin soil of Kansas and God give the victory to the side that is stronger in numbers, as it is in the right!" Eli Thayer, a New England abolitionist, contended that the best way to wipe out the "great national curse" was to "go to the prairies of Kansas and show the superiority of the free labor civilization; to go with all our free labor trophies and in a peaceful contest convince every poor man from the South of the superiority of free labor." Thayer claimed that action was the answer rather "than to stay at home and talk of manacles and auction-blocks and bloodhounds. That our work was not to make women and children cry in anti-slavery conventions, by sentimental appeals, BUT TO GO AND PUT AN END TO SLAVERY."[9]

The angry feelings caused by the Kansas-Nebraska Act changed the political landscape. Free-Soilers, Northern Whigs and antislavery Democrats soon fused into a new political organization, the Republican Party. Abraham Lincoln of Illinois, one of the earliest champions of Republican principles, summed up his feelings about the defenders of slavery and the passive defenders of slavery, including those in the recently formed Know-Nothing political party:

> *As a nation, we began by declaring that "all men are created equal." We now practically read it "all men are created equal except negroes." When the Know-Nothings get control, it will read "all men are created equal, except negroes, and foreigners and catholics." When it comes to this I should prefer emigrating to some other country where they make no pretence of loving liberty—to Russia, for instance, where despotism can be taken pure and without the base alloy of hypocrisy.* [10]

The eyes of countless Americans were fixed on the Kansas territory and the attempt to implement popular sovereignty. The stakes were high, and both sides refused to give up without a fight. The free staters feared that if they lost Kansas to slavery, the slave mentality would continue to spread westward. But they fervently hoped that if Kansas were admitted as a free state, slavery would have a hard time spreading farther. All slave owners were well aware that the last thing they wanted was a free state in proximity. [11]

People began to migrate to Kansas almost immediately after news of the passage of the Kansas-Nebraska bill was made official. Abolitionists Eli Thayer, Amos Lawrence and Charles Robinson, among others, helped to fund and promote settlement in the Kansas territory through the New England Emigrant Aid Society (or Company). The New England Emigrant Aid Society was devoted to the abolition of slavery and, more specifically, to resisting its further spread west. Groups such as these were prepared to go to the Kansas territory and make a stand ideologically and physically if needed.

Although this group of settlers became quite celebrated, others began to pour into Kansas as well. A large portion of the Free-Soil settlers hailed from midwestern states like Ohio, Indiana, Illinois, Iowa and Missouri. Southerners and proponents of slavery claimed that northerners were attempting to "abolitionize" the West. The first territorial governor, Andrew Reeder, a Pennsylvanian, was left with the difficult charge of keeping the peace. Clashes occurred almost immediately over land claims, town sites and water rights. In the first election held in Kansas, in the fall of 1854, proslavery men were determined to make a stand. On election day, more than 1,700 armed Missourians crossed the border to vote in Kansas. These proslavery advocates were dubbed "border ruffians" by the free state press, and their votes helped send a proslavery delegate to Washington.

Physical violence and threats became commonplace in the Kansas territory, and any attack was usually followed by a retaliatory strike. The focus of anger for many proslavery Missourians was the town of Lawrence, which reeked of abolitionism and change. Free blacks walked up and down its streets. Douglas County and other places in northeast Kansas became stations on the Underground Railroad, conducting slaves from bondage to freedom. In 1855, it appeared that a shooting war was about to develop when a free state settler was killed; two sides quickly emerged. Opposing forces met on both sides of the Wakarusa River and were only convinced not to fight when Territorial Governor Wilson Shannon, successor to Governor Andrew Reeder, along with free staters Charles Robinson and former U.S. congressman from Indiana Jim Lane struck a last-minute compromise. The episode, referred to as the "Wakarusa War," served notice that both sides were willing to use violence on behalf of their respective causes.

The spring of 1856 demonstrated that Wakarusa and the tension of 1855 were only the beginning of a crisis. In the strictest of terms, if Bleeding Kansas could be boiled down to one period or year, that year would be 1856. In May 1856, an army of seven hundred proslavery men rode into Lawrence and burned, pillaged and destroyed two newspaper offices, the Eldridge "Free State" Hotel and more. The looting went on until dark when finally, drunk and reeling, the border ruffians stumbled out of town. Their route was lit by the flames from homes on top of Mount Oread, including that of prominent free stater and later governor Charles Robinson. The perpetrators of the violence were given heroes' welcomes when they returned home.[12]

The motivation behind Missourians and the proslavery forces was twofold. First, they truly wanted their side to triumph over free staters, and Lawrence was the grand prize, the "abolitionist hellhole" that they desired. Second, Missourians especially were becoming outraged by the activities of free staters who were making forays into Missouri to emancipate slaves. This activity was seen by Missourians as a theft of property. Some free staters took the opportunity to do more than liberate slaves. At least some free staters believed that anything a slave owner possessed had dubious origins, obtained through the sweat or toil of an enslaved human being. The free staters thus justified theft of other personal property as fair payment for the sin of slavery. These "jayhawkers" became as hated by Missourians as the "border ruffians" were hated and feared by Kansans. In either case, the outrages and violence perpetrated by both sides simply exacerbated the entire situation. All too often, innocent civilians with little or no political perspective were caught in the middle.[13]

In May 1856, Charles Sumner, senator from Massachusetts, delivered a vitriolic speech entitled "The Crime Against Kansas." Sumner lashed the South and Missouri with harsh language about how Kansas was being "raped." Included in his speech was a reference to the aged senator from South Carolina, Andrew Butler, who had "read many books of chivalry, and believes himself a chivalrous knight, with sentiments of honor and courage. Of course he has chosen a mistress to whom he has made vows, and who, though ugly to others, is always lovely to him; though polluted in the sight of the world, is chaste in his sight. I mean the harlot slavery."[14]

Two days later, Butler's cousin, South Carolina representative Preston Brooks, entered the Senate chamber after adjournment, approached the desk of Sumner and calmly said, "Mr. Sumner. I have read your speech over carefully. It is a libel on South Carolina, and Mr. Butler, who is a relative of mine." Just as Sumner began to rise, Brooks delivered a slight blow with the end of his cane. Sumner raised his hands in an effort to defend himself, and Brooks began to "rain down blows." To his friends, Brooks had proclaimed in advance that he intended only to flog Sumner, but when the beating was over, he had delivered thirty blows in about one minute. During the assault, Sumner struggled so hard to get out of his seat that "with the pressure of his thighs, he ripped the desk from the floor." Finally, Brooks was pulled away from the nearly unconscious Sumner. Sumner recovered from the beating, but he would not serve in the Senate again for three years. The event angered many northerners but delighted many southerners, who thought that the beating was deserved and would send a message to the antislavery North. Brooks's cane and its remnants became sacred objects.[15]

The sack of Lawrence and the reported beating of Charles Sumner on the Senate floor sent shock waves throughout the nation. To one settler in the Kansas territory, it did much more than shock. John Brown had come to Kansas in late 1855, joining his sons and his sister and brother-in-law, Florella and Samuel Adair. Brown, who had taken a claim near the town of Osawatomie, was an avowed abolitionist. For his entire life, he had wanted to make a stand against the evil of slavery. Soon after his arrival, he witnessed violence and saw firsthand the many proslavery settlers who had come from the south. Like many, he had witnessed the resolve of these settlers. Brown became convinced that physical threat needed to be met with physical threat. He had grown tired of the appeasing and complacent abolitionists who continued only to pray for change. Brown was convinced that more had to be done. After the events of May 1856, an angered Brown snapped.

On the night of May 24, Brown and eight men decided to go on a secret expedition. Their goal was to settle the score in the Pottawatomie valley of Kansas and discourage proslavery sentiment and further settlement. The first target that evening was the cabin of a slavery advocate, James Doyle. One of Brown's men, James Townsley, remembered:

> *The old man Doyle and his two sons were…marched some distance from the house…where a halt was made. Old John Brown drew his revolver and shot…Doyle in the forehead, and Brown's two youngest sons immediately fell upon the younger Doyles with their…swords. One of the young Doyles was stricken down in an instant, but the other attempted to escape, and was pursued a short distance by his assailant and cut down.*[16]

The party continued on that evening, killing two more men, Allen Wilkinson and William Sherman. The work was completed, and Brown believed that he had made a stand for the free state cause. "It has been ordained by the Almighty God, ordained from eternity, that I should make an example of these men."[17]

Within days, search parties were looking for the killers of the five men on the Pottawatomie. A proslavery posse under the command of Henry Clay Pate burned the cabin of John Brown Jr., as well as a store belonging to free stater Theodore Weiner. On June 4, Pate was camped at Black Jack, near Hickory Point. John Brown learned of Pate's location and decided to surprise him. Leading two companies of about thirty-five men, Brown attacked Pate's men at breakfast. After a battle that lasted nearly three hours, Brown's men had begun to withdraw when Brown's unbalanced son Frederick galloped onto the field in full view of Pate and his men, shouting that they were outnumbered. The spectacle of Fred Brown's appearance convinced Pate that reinforcements had arrived. Pate sent out a messenger under a white flag. Within minutes, John Brown was holding a gun to Pate's head, demanding surrender. Pate and his twenty-eight men complied. Remembering the Battle of Black Jack later, Pate said, "I went to take Brown—and he took me."[18]

Within a month, federal troops under the command of Colonel Edwin Sumner had begun to assert control. Free staters had elected their own government, despite the fact that President Franklin Pierce and the U.S. government had declared the existing territorial government valid. As the free state legislature prepared to meet in Topeka, Sumner interrupted the proceedings. He entered the building, took a position on the speaker's platform and declared that while it was "the most painful duty of my whole life," he must "command you to disperse." Sumner assured the legislators that he would use any and all force to comply with his orders. Sumner's actions supported the free state position that the U.S. Army was a weapon of tyranny against free state Kansans. Sumner even came under fire from some members of the Pierce administration who realized that such a demonstrative act gave more favorable media attention to the free state cause.[19]

The intensity of 1856 continued during the next few weeks. A battle at Franklin and at an outpost near Lecompton called Fort Titus showed the divisiveness that pervaded the territory. At Titus, free staters under the command of Samuel Walker were intent on the capture of proslavery leader Henry Titus. Free staters were angered not only by what they believed to be their inability to be involved in the political process but also by the recent arrests of various free state leaders. Titus was defeated and captured. As Titus and his men surrendered, Samuel Walker remembered:

> [Titus] *was all covered with blood, having received several severe wounds. The moment he was seen a hundred rifles were leveled at his head and he shook like a leaf. Seeing me on my horse he cried, "For God's sake, Walker, save my life! You have a wife and children; so have I. Think of them and save me." He was a pitiable object and his appeal touched me.... I took Titus into the stable. The men were intent on his life, and I had to knock one fellow down to keep him from shooting the poor wretch on the spot.*[20]

On August 30, a proslavery band numbering in the hundreds attacked the town of Osawatomie, home of John Brown and many of his followers. This time, Brown was outmanned, and the town was soon in flames. Brown's son Fred was killed, as were several other free state men. For Brown, who escaped with many of his men, the attack on Osawatomie was a turning point. He knew that his work was larger than the Kansas territory. As he looked at the burning town, he reportedly remarked, "God sees it.... I have only a short time to live—only one death to die, and I will die fighting for this cause. There will be no more peace in this land until slavery is done for. I will give them something else to do than extend slave territory. I will carry this war into Africa."[21]

Kansas continued to bleed for the next few years. Intimidation, violence, political threats and grandstanding were commonplace. By 1858, John Brown was making national news on a much larger scale, having moved his struggle back east, and by 1859, he was planning a raid that would link his name forever with the start of the Civil War. In the territory, however, things were beginning to stabilize by 1859. Free staters were gaining ground in most areas, and it was increasingly apparent that Kansas could enter the Union as a free state. As the election year of 1860 approached, a Republican candidate from Illinois came to the Kansas territory. Lincoln arrived on December 1, 1859. Ironically, the very next day, John Brown was hanged in Virginia for attempting to rescue slaves at Harper's Ferry.

In Elwood, Lincoln addressed forty people at the Great Western Hotel, commenting that while he thought Brown "of great courage and unselfishness," Brown was wrong in spilling blood. Lincoln said that the ballot box and fair elections were the best ways for the Kansas territory to end the violence. Lincoln also spoke in Troy and Leavenworth, spending five days traveling in the northeast corner of the territory. In Leavenworth, Lincoln spoke to about four hundred. The biggest city in Kansas at the time, Leavenworth was still in many ways a primitive place on the frontier and certainly very different than towns in the East or even the midwestern states. While residents remembered Lincoln's time in Kansas for the rest of their lives, at the time of his visit, few knew that within eleven months he would be the choice for president of the United States. Even among Republicans, he was a dark horse candidate, and most Kansans favored New York senator William Seward, who had been an outspoken advocate of free institutions and the free state movement.[22]

Kansas entered the Union as a free state on January 29, 1861. "Bleeding Kansas" had come to an end, but the nation was on the brink of division and Civil War. As the war escalated in 1861, much of the nation was surprised by the anger, the hatred and the resolve of both the North and the South. To people of the Kansas-Missouri border, though, the dissension was no shock. They had watched its evolution for nearly seven years. Christian Isely and Elise Dubach were among those hardened people of the border who had watched the violence, the hardships and the random terror. Like so many people in the region, by the start of the Civil War, they had already formulated opinions and chosen sides.

CHAPTER 3

"I WILL NOW FIGHT FOR MR. LINCOLN"

In the spring of 1856, after spending the previous year in St. Joseph with his brother, Benjamin Dubach set out to establish a claim in the Kansas territory. Although much of the good farmland near the Kansas-Missouri border was already taken, Dubach found a farmer in Doniphan County who was willing to relinquish his claim for $100.00. The Dubach family still had to live on the claim and pay the government fee of $1.25 per acre. The family took possession in March, and for the next three years, Elise was both mother and housekeeper to her father and two brothers.

Elise also witnessed firsthand the violence that was raging along the Kansas-Missouri border. She recounted that among farmers in Doniphan County, there was little animosity over the issue: "No neighbor ever insulted us for being foreigners. Neither did they hate us because we were for a free state while some of them were for making Kansas a slave state." Elise remembered that some of their proslavery neighbors protected the Dubach family from the Missouri raiders. One night in 1856, Jim Boston knocked on the Dubach family door. Since her father could speak little English, Elise took the message. "The border ruffians are coming over tomorrow to drive out the abolitionists," he said. "Put a white cloth on your chimney, and you will be safe." The Dubach family did as they were told, and they along with many Free-Soil neighbors were not molested because all had shown the white cloth.[23]

Elise wrote that "the feeling of neighborliness is stronger among farmers than among city dwellers, but it was especially strong in pioneer communities."

Due to the fact that many of the Dubachs' neighbors came from all parts of the country, Elise was a witness to varied political opinions. Two families who were dear friends, the Hutchinsons and the Bostons, hailed from the mountains of eastern Kentucky. They came to Kansas partly because of the chance at free land but also to escape competition with slavery. "It has been so long since slave days," Elise wrote, "we have forgotten that the institution was a handicap to white men as it was to negroes. Poor white people of the South who had no slaves were forced to compete in the labor market with slave labor." Because of this, Elise stated, such Southerners were opposed to the extension of slavery into Kansas.

After three years on the Kansas claim, the life of Elise Dubach changed again. Benjamin Dubach remarried, and a stepmother along with five more children became part of the Dubach family. Uncle Christian and his wife, Christine, invited Elise to come live with them in St. Joseph. Christian and Christine Dubach ran a boardinghouse, and Elise became a part of their working family. St. Joseph was a good-sized community by frontier standards, boasting eleven thousand people, including two thousand slaves. The railroad had come to St. Joseph, and it was an important outpost for many people heading west. Elise recalled that in 1859, Horace Greeley, the editor of the *New York Tribune*, came to St. Joseph to give a speech. Later that same year, Abraham Lincoln passed through the city on his way to Elwood, Kansas, to give a speech in favor of admitting Kansas as a free state.[24]

Elise's new residence and occupation gave her the opportunity to come into contact with people of varying backgrounds and places. The rules at the boardinghouse were especially stiff. "We neither served liquor nor permitted anyone who was even slightly intoxicated to enter our house. This enhanced our reputation and brought us only sober men." On one particular occasion, a drunk presented himself at the boardinghouse during the dinner hour. "He was a big man; and since I was little more than five feet tall, I had to throw my head back to look up at him." The man glaringly dared Elise to throw him out. Elise opened the door and declared, "That place was made by the carpenter for you to get out." Without any further protest, the man exited. Elise supposed that many of the sober men would have rushed to her aid had the man become violent. After her fierce stand, many of the thirty or so men in the house praised Elise loudly, including Christian H. Isely. "He was a nephew of my stepmother's first husband, but until that time, aside from saying 'Good Morning' or 'Please, give me a second cup of coffee,' he had never noticed me, nor I him. But on this particular occasion, after supper had been finished, Christian said 'You are surely a brave girl,' and there was an especial fervor in his tone." It was not the first time a man had spoken kindly or paid attention to Elise, but as she would say later, "I spurned them all, that is all until C.H. Isely came upon the scene."[25]

Following Christian's kind comments, he and Elise began to see more of each other. Christian later confessed to Elise the feelings he had been afraid to share: "My whole heart was smitten with the tenderst affection towards You my love…. I wished to talk to you; but could I do it—no I could not, for I was affraid some jealous heart might overhear us; and so I had to suppress my feelings." Christian was already convinced of his devotion and love for Elise. "I cannot withhold my feelings from you…. You and you alone—on this earth possess my heart—my heart beats soly for thee—and thee alone it loves—O would to God that I could have Your heart in return." Christian wished to know Elise's heart, so he could then share more openly with her. "Should it be my lot to find favor in Your sight I would then endeavor to find an opportunity to speak to You privately." Christian, after sharing a poem he wrote for Elise, concluded by saying, "I would be very glad if [I] could know something of your sentiments."[26]

Christian believed in self-improvement and worked hard at humbling himself as a person. This humble spirit was a reflection of his strong religious convictions. Obviously, Christian was interested in Elise from the outset, and he certainly entertained thoughts of marriage. However, apparently because of a lack of income or his own feelings of unworthiness, he hesitated to rush into matrimony. Surely, Elise could have played a major role in the decision as well. At the time of their meeting, Elise was about seventeen years old and Christian thirty-one. In a letter dated April 29, 1859, Christian pledged his devotion and apologized for his behavior at times. "If I could do anything to make you happy I would do anything in my power, even if it was to occupy my whole life to do it in; for I think if any person deserves to be happy, you do." And then, apologetically, Christian stated that although occasionally "I don't appear to be friendly to your eyes, it is very often, my Dear, that my lips do not speak a friendly word to You; but nevertheless speaks the heart volumes of gratitude and tender affections for you, and for you alone."[27]

In late 1859 or early 1860, Elise moved back home with her father, stepmother and siblings. The farm in Doniphan County was near Willow Dale and was referred to by Christian and Elise as the old Willow Dale home. Elise wrote a letter to Christian on March 19, 1860: "You told me to remember you in prayer. I do. O! Christian—but it seems to me that nobody needs more to be remembered in prayer than I do. I am such [a] poor sinfull creature that sometimes I think myselfs no longer worthy of God's mercy."

Humility and improvement were always core values to Christian and Elise. In addition to discussing religious matters, Elise noted, "You wish me to write much but I am such a poor writer. I pieced a quilt for you and we are going to quilt it next week if we can."[28]

On June 4, 1860, Christian wrote in his diary of his depression regarding both temporal and spiritual things. Elise was his utmost concern. "Why should I not be concerned about the eternal welfare of her whom I love dearer than my own life. Having also been out of imployment—having indeavored and tried my utmost to get imployment but found none greatly increased my sorrow." Indeed, the lack of employment and his debts "made this a most doleful day to me, a day so dark that I shall never forget it."[29]

Elise not only held Christian's heart and thoughts, she could also lift his spirits with kind words. On August 6, 1860, she wrote, "[A]lthough we can not see and speak to each other very often we can write to each other and if we can't do that we can think of each other." Christian, on the other hand, remained consumed with self-doubt. "O my sweetest Love I am intirely unworthy of your conduct towards me, unworthy of your Love, your affection, your Kindness." He consistently battled sin and at times had not behaved properly. "O sweetest Love if you will forgive me I will promise you that I will not come over to see you till I am a better man and till I have a better heart—to deserve to be in your ever precious company." He next suggested that he did not deserve her love or affection. "O my dearest darling Love.—don't you think you had better withdraw yourself, yes your own noble self, from one that deserves so little and try your lot with some better one—and let me die a broken hearted death, for that is all I deserve anyway?" Christian ended the letter by stating that he was seriously trying to change. "I have prayed more than ever before in such short a time. Last Saturday I spent the whole afternoon in my little room, in reading, praying and weeping, when evening came I was quite fatigued, but felt very happy."[30]

Christian and Elise continued to write and see each other as often as they could. Exactly when Christian proposed is unclear. As the year 1861 dawned, the idea of marriage was apparently getting closer. Elise recollected that Christian was "industrious, a great reader, a church-going man. He neither smoked nor drank. When he proposed marriage I accepted." After Elise accepted, Christian, a contracting carpenter by trade, "built a cottage on Frederick Avenue and around it planted twenty-four fruit trees. He made most of the furniture and I bought dishes and other things for the home where I was to be a happy mistress."[31]

The marriage took place at the parsonage of the Sixth Street Presbyterian Church in St. Joseph, Missouri, on May 31, 1861. A close family friend, Reverend John G. Fackler, conducted the ceremony. Elise wore a wool and silk dress with black and wine-colored checks, trimmed with a lace collar. The skirt was worn over hoops. Elise's bonnet was of white leghorn. "It had a bow at the crown, flowers on either side, and wide plaid ribbons which were tied in a bow under her chin." Christian wrote a letter on their wedding day, recording "[h]ow sweet every word sounded that was spoken by our worthy Pastor. This was because we tried to live humbly before God, and no guilty conscience reproved us." The letter also expressed how much Elise meant to him. "Her love has at all times been a firm and perpetual devotion." Christian concluded with a prayer that with God's help, he felt strong enough to discharge his duties as a faithful husband. Elise "lacked three weeks of being nineteen, and my husband had just celebrated his thirty-third birthday. Our wedding was set for Friday, because the bridegroom wished to prove to his mother that Friday was as good a day as any on which to begin a new venture."[32]

Six weeks before the marriage of Christian and Elise, the Civil War began with the attack on Fort Sumter, South Carolina. Maybe all of the violence along the border had lulled some people into believing that the war could not affect them any deeper. Unfortunately, they were wrong. The Civil War would soon be felt in St. Joseph. The nation and Missouri were split in two, and Christian and Elise Isely found themselves caught in the middle of the approaching storm.

Missouri entered the Union as a slave state in 1821, shortly after the free state of Illinois. By the time of the Civil War, Iowa and Kansas had joined the Union, so Missouri shared three borders with states opposed to slavery. Elise recalled, "Many times had parties from Missouri crossed into Kansas on various hostile errands; and once a band of Kansans, boldly entering St. Joseph at night, delivered one of their citizens from jail where he had been sentenced for conducting fugitive slaves to freedom contrary to both state and national law. These bold Kansans escaped unharmed in rowboats to Elwood." The last episode to which Elise alluded was the rescue of Dr. John Doy. Doy and his son, Charles, had attempted to rescue thirteen slaves and take them to Nebraska when they were captured twelve miles outside of Lawrence and taken to Weston, Missouri, on the charge of abducting slaves. Trials were held in nearby St. Joseph, and while Charles was released, John was held over and sentenced to serve five years in the penitentiary. Several friends rescued him from the St. Joseph jail on September 23, 1859, much to the chagrin and embarrassment of his captors. Certainly, these occurrences had a profound impact on the people of the border.[33]

Once the war erupted, Missourians were divided. Both sides alleged that they were more numerous. A nineteenth-century Missouri historian calculated that "[a]lthough the Breckenridge, or Southern rights men, were in a minority in the State even when compared with the supporters of Douglas, in the legislature they outnumbered either of the other parties." Due to the union of both the Democratic factions, a proslavery candidate was elected as speaker of the legislature. The end result was that Missourians were arguing in their backyards and within the legislature about whether they should secede. In a short time, both a pro-Union and a pro-Confederate government existed. Nonetheless, Missouri never officially seceded from the Union. Christian, due to a variety of reasons, hesitated to enlist initially, but he and Elise did have strong views. "My husband and I were both against slavery," she wrote, "although public opinion in St. Joseph was largely favorable to the institution." Only about one man in ten owned slaves in Missouri, so this approval or sentiment in favor of slavery puzzled Elise. "In St. Joseph there were only two slaves for each nine white people. But the slave owners were the men of wealth. They dominated the press, the pulpit, and other fountains of public opinion." It was a topic that Christian, too, wrote about often in his letters and diaries. Elise summarized their feelings by stating that "[n]ot only did I regard slavery as harmful to the free working man, but I had been taught that slavery was a sin. This view was strengthened by some of my close-up contacts with the system."[34]

One incident made a special impact on Elise. She witnessed a black woman being sold from a scaffolding within a block of her uncle's home in St. Joseph. Elise wrote that the scene was reminiscent of *Uncle Tom's Cabin*. When the auctioneer's hammer fell, announcing that the sale had been made, "the buyer led his slave to his carriage and drove away at a trot. The woman, realizing that she would never see her friends again, burst into screaming lamentations." Elise "felt like screaming with her. Of course, we anti-slavery people were against secession and regarded the two issues as one."[35]

St. Joseph was quite evenly divided on the issue of secession. On Saturday, April 20, 1861, six days after the fall of Fort Sumter, a company of thirty-four well-known local residents rode into town. Each rider sported a red shirt, blue cockade and brace of revolvers. A public meeting was to be held that afternoon at the courthouse, and the streets were filled with anxious citizens. Secession flags waved from the windows of residences and businesses in the town. According to Elise, the current was "very overpoweringly secessionward." The mounted men rode leisurely down Felix Street, "bearing the flag and clothed with the insignia of treason, cheered on by crowds of men and boys who shouted for Jeff Davis and groaned for the Union and its defenders." At the end of the street, the riders hoisted a Southern banner. A young lawyer then warned that the flag unfurled that day in St. Joseph would never descend "except drenched in fraternal blood."[36]

The battle for St. Joseph was far from over. That night, a Kansas boy about eighteen years of age crossed the Missouri River, climbed the flagpole, pocketed the flag and safely returned to Elwood. On Sunday morning, the rebels were incensed that their flag did not still wave over St. Joseph and that its descent was not attended by a bloody baptism. A few weeks later, a new postmaster appointed by new president Abraham Lincoln made his appearance in town. After being properly installed, he unfurled a Union flag from the roof of the building. The sight of the flag produced excitement among the people. Soon, a noisy, angry crowd collected around the building. Shouting and yelling, several clambered onto the roof, "hauled down the flag, tore it into shreds, and trampled it in the mud and mire of the gutters of Francis Street." It was then discovered by the secessionists that some loyal Germans had raised the Union banner over Turner Hall. The mob marched to the hall and ordered the flag be taken down. It was promptly lowered. The next day, the city council met and passed an ordinance forbidding the raising of any flag within the corporate limits of St. Joseph.

The citizens of St. Joseph who sided with the Union requested military aid, and in the first week of June, they got their wish. Captain Alfred Sully and several hundred Federal soldiers arrived in St. Joseph, precipitating a retreat of the secessionists to outlying areas. Shortly after Captain Sully arrived, he unfurled the Stars and Stripes from the dome of the Patee House. As the flag swung out, soldiers and citizens shouted their approval, and a band struck up "The Star-Spangled Banner." Townspeople joined in with drums and fifes, and a wave of emotion soon led to roofs all over the city displaying the national colors. When asked by the marshal and a posse of twelve men to obey the laws of the city and strike his colors, Sully refused, stating that his business in St. Joseph was to defend the flag of his country. He had unfurled it, and when it descended, he and his command would fall with it. The next evening, the ordinance was repealed. The presence of the Federal troops was not a welcome sight to all the residents of St. Joseph. Often citizens of the area who were loyal to the Union had to cross the Missouri River and enlist in the Kansas town of Elwood.[37]

As the summer of 1861 wore on, Christian and Elise settled into their new home. The news of the war was discussed at church, in stores and on the street. It was difficult to avoid the debate and even more difficult not to formulate some sort of opinion. Before the Civil War, Christian apparently was not interested in politics. During the presidential election of 1856, he confided to his brother back in Ohio, "One person cannot accomplish anything; you have to give the reins to the mass of the people. You cannot influence them with excitement and quarreling. As for myself I partake very little in the election." Christian supported the Northern Democrat Stephen A. Douglas in the election of 1860. Nonetheless, in light of all the violence and conflict in and around St. Joseph, Christian decided on May 6, 1861, to write to President Abraham Lincoln.[38]

Christian confided that it was "[w]ith a bleeding heart do I think of the dangers that are surrounding our heretofore so happy and prosperous Land and Nation." He pledged his undying devotion to both the president and the nation and stated that the traitors would never win because "we have justice, right, the glorious cause, etc., and above all the Allmighty…on our side." It would not be an easy task, but ultimately "those poor deluded brethren who are now rebeling against us, will share those blessings, and be happy with us." Christian claimed that all Americans had sinned against God and that all Americans should humble themselves and seek divine guidance.[39]

Christian pleaded with the new president to seek God's guidance, as George Washington had done. Christian believed that Lincoln was also a God-fearing man and that this would be a key to success. Christian then turned his attention to matters closer to home. "I for my part would like to do much for our favored Land and I do not know of any thing whereby I could do more than by fervently praying for it and its Rulers, and I also do it with a cheerful heart every day." Christian related that the secessionists were so numerous in western Missouri that Union men were afraid to express their loyalty. "I have a small house in St. Joe and the worst of [it] is I owe some money on it yet, and to a secessionist at that, but I left every thing commiting it to the care of God, and came over here to Kansas." Christian added that he planned to join a company of Union men. In Kansas, "I know that I am not among traitors, but if [in] Missouri I could not say so." Christian concluded his letter by stating that "I have been a Douglass Democrat and voted for him last fall. But I will now fight for Mr. Lincoln and the administration if necessary."[40]

Although he likely never mailed the letter to President Lincoln, perhaps because he continued to hesitate to enlist, Christian was deeply moved by the events of the war. He felt uncomfortable in St. Joseph and was much more content at Elise's parents' house in Kansas. "The Civil War began six weeks before our marriage," Elise recalled, "but we did not believe it would affect us. For six years war had been waging along the Kansas-Missouri border, so we were accustomed to it." She stated that "Christian followed the news closely and we talked of it with the greatest personal interest." They were not alone.[41]

During the summer of 1861, Christian received correspondence from family and friends in Ohio talking of the war. A letter dated June 23 from a childhood friend, John Kunzli of Winesburg, was laced with patriotic Union feeling. "Dear Friend, Christian Isely, I am happy to hear that you have thus far escaped the evil disposed and Bloodthirsty Secessionists although you have undoubtedly suffered a great deal in a pecuniary matter, by the secession movement. According to the reports...we have reason to hope that the secession cause will soon be crushed in your State." Kunzli related that some of their mutual friends had joined the fight, and he expressed high hopes for Missouri. "I think there is good reason to hope that several of the border Slave States will abolish Slavery soon and if Missouri will abolish slavery she will undoubtedly be one of the first rank States in the Union on account of her center locality." Indeed, Kunzli was convinced that Missouri would be a good place to move the capital of the United States. "It would certainly suit much better than the present location. I think the present war will in great measure purge the Country of old political cliques and treasury suckers."[42]

The first major clash of the Civil War occurred in northern Virginia at the Battle of Bull Run on July 21, 1861. Up until this point, it was assumed by many that the war would be over in a short time, but neither side sensed the resolve of the other to be victorious at all costs. Bull Run demonstrated to Northerners that they were totally unprepared for war. A mere show of their military might and patriotic zeal was not enough to defeat the Southern forces. Union soldiers who had received little training witnessed their friends and comrades being shot and killed. To the horrors of the battle, these untrained soldiers reacted not as fighting men but as scared citizens seeking survival. The Union army was routed and beat a quick path back to Washington.

Bull Run was not only a strong military defeat for the Union in the first major clash of the Civil War, it was also an embarrassment. The cry for new recruits became much more intense. Christian Isely and others watched these developments closely and formulated opinions. His diary and later writings reveal that these changes helped persuade him to get involved. Throughout the summer, Christian wrestled with the difficult decision of war. He was troubled by what was occurring, but like so many others, he could not imagine leaving home and loved ones.

CHAPTER 4

"TO FIGHT FOR A JUST CAUSE"

Christian decided to join the fight in the summer of 1861. The letters and diaries reveal that despite the varying views of his family and some friends, Christian formulated his own opinions and acted accordingly. The sectional conflict came to a head in Missouri on August 10, when Union and Confederate forces clashed near Springfield at Wilson's Creek. Union forces under Nathaniel Lyon were defeated by General Sterling Price in a bloody battle that took the life of General Lyon. At least for a time, it looked as if Missouri might fall to Confederate control. This battle and the casualty reports inspired many men to enlist. Following the carnage at Wilson's Creek, the Unionist citizens of St. Joseph heard more alarming news. It was reported that General Price was marching north toward St. Joseph. Price, a Mexican-American War veteran and prosperous planter of Virginia birth, was one of the most wealthy and influential men in Missouri. Although proslavery in his sentiments, Price had not been a secessionist. Instead, he saw himself as a defender of Missouri against Northern invasion. Price eventually made his way to the river town of Lexington, where he won another victory.[43]

Many years later, Elise Dubach Isely remembered these events in her book, *Sunbonnet Days*. The first disconcerting thing to the Iselys during that tumultuous summer of 1861 were the mixed feelings of many of their friends, as well as the Confederate leanings of many of their fellow church members. Elise wrote that as the rebel troops approached St. Joseph, "several members of our own church quietly departed to the Confederate camp...the St. Joseph recruits took the news to Price that St. Joseph could be captured easily, and a branch of Price's army crossed the One-Hundred-and-Two River and marched on the town. The unionists in St. Joseph were apprised by couriers of the Confederate approach." Of course, this caused excitement to those loyal to the Union. As news of Price's approach spread, "Hundreds of citizens crossed the river; almost every store was closed; and the entire city looked more like a deserted village, than the lively, prosperous St. Joseph of a year previous." Those who fled by rail met with a terrible accident that left eighteen dead. When the surviving passengers arrived back in St. Joseph, most of them were injured to some extent. As the lifeless form of the conductor was removed from the wreckage, a woman sympathetic to the Confederate cause coldly remarked, "No matter, he was but a miserable Abolitionist." Elise remembered that "there was nothing for Christian to do but to find a skiff and row across to Kansas. As an avowed unionist he was in danger. Hundreds of Union men of military age also fled."[44]

Elise described the gloomy sights and sounds of the next few days. "Soon after Christian had gone, I saw the Confederates arriving," equipped with every kind of gun. Most of them wore jeans and were "unshorn" country boys. Some of the invaders were St. Joseph boys. While they looked disorganized, Elise claimed that "we people of the border knew that every man and boy of them could hit a squirrel in the eye at the distance of the top of a hickory tree." The situation was tense. Elise remembered that "frightful stories were circulated regarding our conquerors. I was told by the extended neighbors that the unshorn Missouri boys would rob us, burn our houses, and that women would be unsafe." Elise did not want to abandon her home, so she took her hatchet to bed with her at night. No significant acts of violence or looting were perpetrated, fortunately, and the rebel raid was of a short duration because "as soon as the news that St. Joseph had been taken was telegraphed to Iowa, five regiments of Iowa boys marched upon us." When the Union soldiers approached the town, the Confederates "skedaddled" in quick order, some of the Iowa boys complaining that they could not get near enough to shoot at their coattails. A short time later, Kansas jayhawkers rode into town to harass disloyal merchants. According to a local historian, the town of St. Joseph became a "shuttle-cock, and [was] thoroughly battered between Missouri thieves and Kansas 'hawks.'"[45]

The Confederate attack on St. Joseph had a profound impact on many of its citizens, including Christian Isely. According to Elise, "It was no longer an abstract question of slavery or secession, but a personal question. Our home was in Missouri. If the south should win, it meant that we would no longer be citizens of the United States, which I had learned to love and which was the only country my husband had known; Missouri would go to the victor and that would make us foreigners to our adopted Fatherland." Christian was increasingly convinced that he had to enlist. On September 10, Elise recorded in her diary Christian's first attempt to enlist in the Union army. "Today has been a day of deep sorrow and mourning to me my dear husband has left me for the field of battle. The secesh troops have also come in our City today. It has also been raining nearly the whole day."[46]

Christian had apparently made up his mind to enlist. In the meantime, he wrote a letter to his mother and sister back in Ohio. Christian was clearly caught up in the emotions of the preceding months, noting, "A bunch of young Rebels took their stand against me by making me the tool for their dirty Work, and I just had to take it. But since then God's hand has found them all, and they all got what was coming to them. They all got twice as much as they were able to do to me." It is unknown what exactly happened. Since Christian refers to them as "young Rebels," it seems that they were aware Christian was a free stater, and he was possibly roughed up a bit. Christian also shared his thoughts about joining the military. "My dear Wife as myself prays Daily to our Father in heaven, that he may let us know his Will, even to go to the Battlefield, as I am not able to find another way out as to fight for our bleeding Country. That should give you all the Assurance that I am willing to give all I have, my life—that you all may be saved." Christian related to his mother and sister the terrible anxiety that existed in western Missouri. After mentioning that the "[11th] Regiment of Illinois and 2 Kansas Regiments came to St. Joseph and cleaned up," Christian pointedly remarked that he was most moved by the arrival of the 39th Ohio Regiment. "How ashamed I was of myself to see that the boys of Ohio were so willing to give even [their] lives just to protect our State! And now I will have no more excuses and I do hope that you all will let me go now with your Blessings." As for Elise, Christian told his family to not worry—she was a strong woman. She and Christian occasionally shed tears, but both were determined and resolute. Moreover, Christian remarked, if Elise were a boy, she would most certainly be a soldier by then.[47]

Christian's brother Henry wrote a letter the same day from the family home in Winesburg, Ohio. Henry's perspective on the Civil War was very different from that of Christian's. Henry wrote that the cries for war were being spread with the "rapidity of electricity." Those who do not declare themselves wholly for the war effort "threaten to make stretch hemp." Henry related a few cases in which two men were threatened with being shot or lynched, but the deed was not carried out. Henry noted that those who were crying for war were not willing to enlist. For his part, Henry pledged his devotion to the "union of hearts, the union of states and the union of lands forever." While Henry stopped short of trying to dissuade Christian from joining the army, he concluded by remarking that "the news that you are going to War caused great sensation in our family which I think is expressed better by the rest of the family in their immediate answers than I can represent it." Henry disclosed the mixed feelings among Christian's own family. The term "Copperhead" describes Northerners who were against the war. Some members of the Isely family living in Ohio had Copperhead leanings, much to Christian's and Elise's disliking.[48]

Christian Isely did not share his family's doubts about the Union war effort. He had made his decision, discussed it with Elise and told his family. The time for action had come. "Having a dear brother in law and two dear cousins in the U.S. service, I concluded also to inlist for the purpose of joining them if it was possible." Christian's subsequent diary entries reveal his innermost feelings. On October 7, he "went to the recruiting office with the strong desire to inlist into the U.S. service but found the recruiting officer absent. The morning was exceedingly bright and beautiful." Two days later, Christian "inlisted for U.S. service and was sworn in by Hugh Cameron at St. Joseph, Mo. afterward invoked a blessing." The following day, Christian fully realized that he would be separated from Elise for an undetermined amount of time. As was always

Christian H. Isely, circa 1863. *Courtesy the Isely family.*

the case, Christian turned to his faith to relieve his anxiety and apprehensions. He reflected in his diary a few days later that he and Elise were "quite resigned and composed."[49]

Christian was scheduled to depart for Fort Leavenworth and be mustered officially into service. On October 17, Christian recorded in his diary that "sadness has been on my mind all day thinking all the while, the parting hour will soon arrive to leave my Wife probably never to see her again." The following day, "The parting scene occurred today which was so touching that it might have melted rocks, but nevertheless, we have been composed and resigned and commited our selves to the care of God." This was a period of emotional turmoil, and Christian's diary in the last week of October reflected these extremes. "My soul was happy in me today, also my body was full of life thinking that I am going forth to fight for a just cause." In Christian's mind at this point, the cause was both the defense of the Union and ridding his country of the evil of slavery. As did many of the people of the border, Elise and Christian saw the two issues as interrelated. A few days later, Christian received a letter from Elise that "made my heart rejoice, but it turned into sadness after reading it." On October 29, he recorded, "Today I was marched with 9 others up to the Fort and were musterd into the U.S. service for 3 years or during the war unless sooner discharged." Although the official regimental designation was not conferred until March 1862, Christian was mustered into the 2nd Kansas Cavalry, Company F.[50]

Christian was not alone in deciding that the time had come to fight in the Civil War. Elise's seventeen-year-old brother, Adolph, also enlisted. Elise said that men of both Northern and Southern inclinations were joining only a few miles apart. Those supporting the Union enlisted within the city limits of St. Joseph, while those who wanted to join General Sterling Price's army had to go only a few miles east of the city to enlist. Elise expressed regret that she, too, could not fight. "There came into the hearts of all of us the feeling that no sacrifice would be too great for the cause. This feeling swept the border, inspiring people with sacrificial spirit. All that counted was the war. Friends, family, and home were of secondary importance." As Christian readied himself for departure, his pastor, John Fackler, remarked that he hoped no stray bullet would strike him, for "I know that no straight one will." Elise sat for a daguerreotype. "It was the first time I had posed for my portrait and since instantaneous photography had not yet been imagined, I had to hold myself almost breathless for three minutes while the impression was slowly formed." The finished picture was placed in a velvet-lined case, and Christian carried it in the blouse of his uniform throughout the war. After Christian left their St. Joseph home, Elise recalled that she went inside and gave vent to her feelings, and "then I seated myself at the window and looked after you till you had disapeared over the hill and then I could not keep my eyes from that direction in the hope of seeing you again, but in vain." As time passed, Elise noted it was "as if in a dream I am watching the return of my Christian but it is as you say a great blessing to have a Friend above who is ever present and to whom we can pour out the feelings of our heart at any time."[51]

Elise Dubach Isely, circa 1863. *Courtesy the Isely family.*

Christian's company was quartered near Fort Leavenworth in northeast Kansas, at an area known as Camp Lincoln. Founded in March 1828 on the left bank of the Missouri River and within twenty miles of the Little Platte River, Fort Leavenworth became the main depot and cavalry supply station for all military establishments in the West following the Mexican-American War. Camp Lincoln was established at the start of the Civil War. It served as a reception and training station where Union volunteers were mustered in, equipped and prepared for battle. Repeatedly during the course of the conflict, it was reported that Missourians under Sterling Price planned to attack Fort Leavenworth. Soldiers at the fort were often kept on a vigilant guard.[52]

The delivery of mail during this period was frustratingly inconsistent. Christian often wrote three or four letters only to have Elise receive one or two. Likewise, this occurred with the letters Elise mailed. On November 10, Christian penned a letter that detailed his first two weeks in the service. Christian reported that his company had good tents and a pair of warm blankets apiece. He had attended church, taken communion and heard a moving story about loyalty and patriotism. Many soldiers of the 2nd Kansas were present at the service, including Major William F. Cloud, Christian's commanding officer. Christian stated in this letter that Southerners accused Northerners of preaching politics from the pulpit, but he believed that these accusations were untrue. Instead, he maintained, they preached that all Americans, North and South, had sinned and that all should be repentant before a Holy God. Hypocritically, Southerners were offended at this type of preaching, Christian remarked, because "[t]hey see the mite in the brothers eye, but are not aware of the beam in their own. They consider us vile sinners because we are loyal to the best government that ever was known on Earth." Christian added that Southerners should judge not lest they be judged.

Christian told Elise not to trouble herself with his needs and then turned his discussion to camp conditions and his many concerns for Elise. He missed her terribly. "You are often floating before me, in a most beautiful vision even far more sublime than in the days of my wooing for your noble heart. Tears have often gushed to my eyes since I am away from you." Christian also regretted that "I have not been kinder to you, and that I have not regarded you better for your unselfish kindness that you have shown unto me." Christian again turned to his faith and concluded in a hopeful tone, "I think these trials are as good schooling for us both, though our path may be thorny and our tears many and large, yet are we accomplishing an end which leads us to the joys of the heavenly climes, where happiness have no limits…. that we may only be profited by every trial that we have to encounter is my desire and sincere prayer."[53]

Christian found out early that the "hardship of soldiering consisted of more than fighting the enemy. He was unfortunate in that he had enlisted in the company of Captain Hugh Cameron." Cameron, according to Elise, was "a peculiar man, who had settled in the free-state town of Lawrence in the early Kansas territorial days. Although he rated himself as a free-state man, he had alienated the regard of his party as early as 1855 by accepting a commission as justice of the peace from the pro-slavery legislature, which usurped the government of Kansas during the first years of territorial government." Free staters referred to this early territorial government as the "bogus" legislature, feeling that it was not representative of the settlers of Kansas territory because of fraudulent voting by Missourians. It was Cameron who had issued the warrant for the arrest of a free state settler by the name of Jacob Branson. This arrest helped to precipitate the bloodless "Wakarusa War" of 1855. Still, as the Civil War broke out, Cameron "managed to obtain a commission to recruit a company for the Second Kansas Cavalry, reorganized to take the place of the Second Kansas Infantry, a ninety-day regiment that had been cut to pieces at Wilson's Creek. Unable to recruit a company in Lawrence, Cameron opened a recruiting office in St. Joseph."

Elise wrote that the idea of Christian enlisting in a Kansas regiment, "which had just been admitted to the Union as a state, and which had been engaged in a war against slavery for six years, appealed to Christian's romantic spirit." In St. Joseph, Cameron assured prospective recruits that officers would be elected after the company was recruited to full strength. That, of course, meant to the men that each officer would be voted on. Therefore, according to Elise, while Christian had no desire for a commission, he at least believed that someone other than Cameron would be elected captain. But it was not to be—Cameron had already obtained his commission. "When the recruits reported for duty at Fort Leavenworth, instead of being called on to nominate officers, as was the practice in many other companies, they were curtly ordered to fall in." Not only did Cameron exercise his new privilege of rank, but he also took special interest in reading various selections of military law to the men of the 2nd Kansas. Elise wrote that Cameron "seemed to take delight in reading the penalties, and placed much more emphasis on the word 'death' whenever it occurred in the reading." The men were resentful, and Cameron responded with discipline and rigor. Christian witnessed men being cruelly punished for minor offenses, "hung up by their thumbs until their toes partly rested on the floor, or to be bucked and gagged." Christian had been appointed corporal and occasionally was detailed to make arrests. Often pleading for leniency, he quickly got in the bad graces of Cameron.[54]

Christian's introduction to military life was very likely not what he had expected. As Christian and Elise's letters and diaries show, he desired very much to serve and do his part on the field of battle. Instead, he was destined to spend a good bit of time at inactive posts, doing garrison duty and serving in a field hospital. The war was really just beginning. How long it would last, and what role Christian and Elise Isely would play, was yet to be determined.

When Christian was mustered into service on October 29, 1861, the original unit designation was the 12th Kansas Infantry. That designation was changed to 9th Kansas Infantry and then finally the 2nd Kansas Cavalry in March 1862. Because of this fluid situation in the winter of 1861–62, Christian and his unit were in a bit of limbo. Often many of these somewhat "unattached" units were sent to perform guard and/or patrol duties.[55]

Christian received a letter, shortly after being mustered in, from his cousin, John F. Ozenberger, a saddler at Fort Scott in the 5th Kansas Cavalry, Company B, who later served in Company A. Also serving in the same regiment was Ozenberger's brother, Willie, and Adolph Dubach, the brother of Elise. Ozenberger expressed his wish that Christian could be transferred to their unit and then described the indignation at the activities of some jayhawkers, claiming that they had confiscated as much Union property as rebels and that they had made a clean sweep of blacks in Missouri. Ozenberger informed Christian that Adolph had improved in health but was still weak and sick at the hospital. Many Civil War soldiers found themselves fighting various diseases rather than the enemy. Apparently, Adolph fell ill in November 1861.[56]

Meanwhile, Christian wrote an interesting and eventful letter to Elise. An Indian agent at the fort requested a military escort for the purpose of making a payment to a group of Delaware Indians. Christian informed Elise that twenty-eight men volunteered for duty. After a journey that lasted from noon until near dark, they arrived at their destination and pitched tents. Christian reported that some of the Indians were drunk and became troublesome. "One of them wanted to get into the Council house and as he found that he could not get [in], he shot through the door and knocked a window in." The Indian was soon corralled, and things quieted down until the following evening, a Sunday, when some of the Indians became intoxicated again. The soldiers had been instructed to let no drunks inside of the yard, and several attempted to restrain one "big raw boned Indian" who entered the camp with a canteen of whiskey. During the scuffle, the Indian stabbed one of the soldiers in the back, and orders were given to take him into custody. Upon seeing this, a female Delaware took an axe and hacked away at the men, cutting one soldier in the forehead and hurting two or three others as well. Christian wrote that "one of our men by this time run the bayonet through the Indian." In the excitement, the vastly outnumbered soldiers were ordered to fall into ranks, with the intention of firing on the Indian camp, when the chief steeped forward and calmed the situation. The injured soldiers were tended to and eventually recovered; it was reported that the drunken Indian later died. That same evening, Major William F. Cloud arrived with twenty-four more men. Christian expressed his joy at the arrival of the reinforcements and noted that Cloud always took a personal interest in his men. Christian also informed Elise that he had met Senator and General James Lane at the fort. "I went to him and introduced myself to him and talked to him." Christian presented the general with a written request by Elise to transfer the Ozenbergers and her brother, Adolph, to Christian's unit. Lane told Christian, "Your wish would be granted. And the boys could be transferred over to our regiment as soon as the two regiments are closer." As to Lane, Christian's only personal comment was that while he said little, it was spoken in kindness. General Lane was a fiery Kansan who stood unequaled in free state and pro-Union support. Appointed as a United States senator in 1861, he shocked many people by getting himself appointed as a brigadier general by President Lincoln. Equipped with this military rank, Lane went about using both his political and military influence from the saddle. No doubt Lincoln was impressed by Lane's quickness to action. Lane could be disliked, but he could not be easily dismissed.[57]

On November 30, 1861, some members of Christian's unit were sent to Weston, Missouri, to "put down rebellion." Christian, however, was detailed to remain with a sick soldier in Leavenworth. On December 2, Christian's "sick man got well, and so I went to camp again." A few days later, Christian was granted a leave to go see Elise in St. Joseph. He recorded in his diary "what a joy it was for us both to meet again and both of us well. We thanked God very much." They were also able to attend church and hear Christian's good friend, John Fackler. "It done my soul good to hear brother Fackler preach again." In a letter written to his parents, Christian and Barbara Ozenberger Isely, on December 15, Christian detailed the situation at home. "St. Joseph is now under strict martial law so nobody can go out of the district without a pass. No pass is given to doubtful persons. Secessionists are arrested and must do work in Ft. Smith or dig entrenchments." Christian stated that on his way home he went through a "secesh gauntlett." He then related his joy at being with Elise. "I had to knock a long time until she was awakened; at first she could not believe it was me—so great was her joy. As painful as our separation was, so happy now was our reunion. We thank God...He throws to us light when we are in darkness; He consoles us when we are downcast."[58]

Within a few days, Christian had to return to Fort Leavenworth. When it became obvious that Christian's regiment would not move south before the spring, he arranged for Elise to join him. Elise revealed that "at Leavenworth there lived a wagon maker, Gottlieb Joss, who had been a schoolmate of Christian in Ohio. Mr. Joss was married and had a family. He and Mrs. Joss invited me to make my home with them where my husband could visit when on leave. I gladly accepted the invitation and went to Leavenworth in

December." Elise described the city of Leavenworth as a "bustling place" when she got there. The city was a rendezvous point for many regiments from Kansas, Nebraska, Missouri and Iowa. The fort served as a sentinel, denying the Confederates access to Kansas and the resources of the West, therefore preventing the breaching of the Union's overland access to California. The area of Leavenworth has been described as an island among a "sea of Copperheads." In addition to its strategic importance, its arsenal possessed huge stores of ordnance.[59]

At Leavenworth, Elise tasted buffalo for the first time, something that she said was a rarity even for plains families of later days. "Mrs. Joss was a good cook and the meat as she served it was the most delicious I have ever tasted. It was more tender and juicy than beef and somewhat fatter." Elise recorded that while many stirring things transpired in and around Leavenworth during the busy winter of 1861–62, her life was quiet. Her "touch with the army was through the visits of Christian on the days when he was on leave." According to Elise, "In spite of an overbearing captain, life in camp was not wholly bad. The lieutenants were kindly men and among the enlisted men there was fine comradeship. All were eager to go to the front." Elise reasoned that "the sooner they departed the sooner they would return."[60]

As the year 1861 came to a close, Christian remained anxious and apprehensive about his future. It was a difficult and cold winter, and many of the men in Christian's unit were detailed to perform guard duties. As was customary, much drilling occurred in the extreme cold, to the dismay of the rank and file. The comfort for Christian was the proximity of Elise. Not only could she visit from time to time, but they could also attend church together. At the end of Christian's diary, he remarked that January 1, 1862, was a memorable day. It was a time of reflection but thanks, too, that all were healthy and that Elise was nearby. Still, he was deeply concerned about his wife. "What will become of her yet ere this struggle is ended, but our trust is in God and I do not think that He will put our souls to shame." Christian recorded in his diary that he had a special time of prayer for all his loved ones, friends and especially his nation. "O that peace may soon be restored to all our once happy borders."[61]

Christian used his free time productively. He was an avid reader and interested in self-improvement. Usually his reading concerned spiritual matters, often books of the Bible or scriptural commentaries. In early January, for example, Christian recorded that he read a religious biography and nearly all of St. John's Revelation. Still, the difficult, cold camp life continued, making its mark on the health of the soldiers. Many men grew ill with colds, coughs and even pneumonia. One acquaintance named Humes passed away, and Christian recorded on January 16 that "today poor Humes gave up his Ghost, poor fellow. I trust he was a child of God." The same day, Christian admitted himself to the hospital. After two days in the hospital and another two weeks of rest and relaxation, Christian was pronounced fit for duty. On his first day back on guard duty, he reported that he "could hardly speak a word loud enough to be heard." Finally, by early February, Christian began to recover his health. The combination of bad weather and ill health made it a difficult winter.[62]

One frequent habit exhibited by the soldiers of the fort that irritated Christian was constant drunkenness. Often detailed as a guard, Christian had to occasionally restrain or help arrest men for being drunk. On January 20, Christian remarked that he dealt with many noisy, drunken prisoners. A few weeks later, Christian reported, "Last night was a riotous one. I had the luck of being on guard, one of our men being nearly killed in the streets by some bull whackers. They were arrested and like to been torn to pieces by our Whiskey pimps." Christian was relieved in February when more units appeared at Fort Leavenworth, many of them veteran and better-drilled units, including the 9th and 13th Wisconsin and the 1st Kansas Infantry. The 1st Kansas was a revered unit, having served gallantly at the Battle of Wilson's Creek. Christian related that they put on a military display that was so grand it made one proud to be a soldier for Uncle Sam.[63]

A recurring theme in Christian's letters and diaries was his concern for Elise's brother, Adolph Dubach. Adolph, only seventeen years of age, enlisted in August 1861 and was attached to the 5th Kansas Cavalry along with the Ozenbergers. In November, Elise and Christian learned that Adolph was ill. The 5th had been on the move much of the fall and spent the remaining winter months in or around Fort Scott. With such distances separating them, the only reports that Christian and Elise received were secondhand accounts from the Ozenberger boys. Christian's diary entry of February 1, 1862, recorded that he "received a letter from cousin Freddie, which reports poor Adolph still sick. It made my dear Wife weep." A week later, Christian requested leave to visit Adolph and the boys of the 5th Kansas. The 13th Wisconsin, then stationed at Fort Leavenworth, was preparing to march to Fort Scott, and Christian saw this as a good opportunity to go with it. His request was denied by the difficult Captain Cameron.[64]

On February 20, a letter arrived from "Cousin Freddie," John F. Ozenberger, containing "the grievious news that poor Adolph was dying." The following day, the news was confirmed in a letter Christian received from someone in Prairie City, Kansas. According to Elise, Christian applied for a leave of absence repeatedly during the month of February, but it was refused each time by Captain Cameron. "Then on February 21 came a letter from Prairie City, Kansas, saying that Adolph was dying." Again, Christian applied for a leave of absence, "this time to Lieutenant French, for the captain was temporarily relieved of command." Cameron was being held in quarters pending a trial on the charge that he had misappropriated soldiers' rations and was selling them. The captain was eventually acquitted, but in the meantime, "Christian obtained leave and set out on horseback for the South."[65]

The journey was a harrowing one, but Christian was determined to get to Adolph as soon as possible. On February 24, he wrote Elise from Prairie City, Kansas. "I found poor Adolph still alive, and as I am told much better than he had been a few days ago—but it is necessary that he is better or he could not have lived to see this hour, it is indeed a wonder that he still lives, nothing saved him but the merciful hand of God." Christian stated that the people of Prairie City were doing everything humanly possible and treating Adolph with kindness. Nevertheless, "There is very little left of him; nothing but bones and skin, nothing looks natural but his calm contented face which is very pale but full yet. His last disease was the lung fever, he lost a great [deal] of blood, and smells awful bad." Christian maintained that "it was poor Adolph's lot to suffer, and preach thus a silent sermon of humility, a meekness & resignation which spoke louder than could be articulated by sounds." Christian wrote, "I asked him whether he had not been sorry that he went to U.S. service. 'Oh no' said he 'I always thought it had to be that way.' I asked whether he had not been homesick, upon this he asked me, 'what good would that have done me; I just took everything as it came and always thought it had to be so.'" Christian realized that although Adolph's life now hung by a thread, there was yet hope for recovery. Both men were affected by their time together. Adolph "wept when he saw me and I felt like it too. It seems to me if he was to die I could hardly live any longer in this world."[66]

In his letter, Christian did not share with Elise the details of his journey to Adolph's side, reporting simply that he had crossed the Kansas River on ice. Years later, Elise recounted that the crossing had been extremely dangerous. Arriving in Lawrence on Saturday evening, Christian learned that the ferryboats would not cross. He also saw the broken-up ice flowing in the river like "swirling ice cakes." On horseback, Christian saw one floe near the shore and "leaped to it, and by tugging at the bridle reins, induced his horse to jump. They floated downstream on that uncertain raft until another floe drew near, and they jumped to that." Elise wrote that Christian and his horse continued to jump from cake to cake until they reached the south bank and were lifted on the shore by two men holding lanterns, who rebuked Christian for performing so foolhardy a feat. Christian resumed the trail the following morning, arriving in Prairie City in a few hours. The arrest of Captain Cameron and Christian's determination to cross the ice-filled river turned out to be significant and fateful occurrences.[67]

Adolph had arrived at Prairie City after a similarly desperate journey. The hardships he had endured the previous winter had been too much to bear. Elise wrote that the news about his regiment was disquieting. They were "without tents. After forced marches the men bivouacked in the snow about an open fire wrapped in sodden blankets, which were too light by night and too heavy by day. The hardships were too much for the constitution of a seventeen-year-old boy." Adolph came down with lung fever, or pneumonia. "Realizing that he could not live, he had bought a horse and buggy and had attempted to drive home. After traveling about seventy-five miles, he collapsed at Prairie City, where he was given shelter by kindly people, who wrote to Christian and also to my father."[68]

Christian's diary entries pick up the rest of the story. On February 24, he recorded, "Adolph seemed to be pretty well this morning but in the evening he was very ill which was quite alarming to me. I do not know what I will [do] if he dies." The following day, Christian wrote, "Adolph was better again this morning, but in the afternoon he commenced spitting blood which made him very weak, but said he did not feel bad. O God save him." Finally on February 26, "ADOLPH went to his HOME! He died between 2 & 3 P.M. His end was PEACE." The following day, Christian recorded, "My heart was full of sadness. My Savior was my only consolation." Elise remembered later how glad she was that Christian managed to arrive several days before Adolph died. Because of this, Adolph "had the satisfaction of feeling the pressure of a brother's hand. He was able to send messages to each of us." Elise's youngest brother, Fred, also attempted to reach Adolph. "My fifteen-year-old brother Fred drove to Prairie City in a wagon. Being delayed at the Kansas River by floating ice, he arrived a half-hour too late to see our brother alive." It was Fred who "took the body home for burial in the churchyard in Doniphan County. Now two of the five who had set out so hopefully from Switzerland seven years before had found graves in America."[69]

Following Adolph's death, Christian had a difficult time resuming military life. "The blow was a hard one to my darling Wife. We were very sad all day. I had a strong desire to be out of the army." Surely, Christian asked why this young patriotic lad's life had ended so abruptly. The weather, the trip and the heartbreak took a toll on Christian. Upon his return, he was assigned to a horse herd detail. Elise noted that "one night in March came a blizzard and the poor horse-herders suffered so terribly from exposure that Christian became desperately ill." Repeatedly in his diary, Christian recorded that his health was feeble, and he was sad and gloomy. On March 18, a doctor advised Christian to admit himself to a field hospital. He remained there for six weeks. He described his condition as painful coughing and feeling very weak. On March 25, battling depression and ill health, Christian confided in his diary, "Who O God art thou pressing so heavy on me—My poor Wife came to see me—but little had I to say to cheer her weeping heart." A day later, Christian added, "Last night I was more composed again. I had sweet thoughts about my poor wife…. O Lord forsake us not in the hour of trial."[70]

While Christian was ill, his regiment moved south to Fort Scott and then into Missouri. When he recovered, Christian was attached to the post artillery at Fort Leavenworth. During this period, Elise learned that she was pregnant. Christian expected to be sent south to rejoin his unit, but the orders did not come for some time. In early April, he was detailed to perform nursing duties in a specific ward with a certain group of soldiers. Christian's diary entries related some of his experiences, including occasionally difficult encounters with fellow soldiers, interspersed with news of the war. On April 11, he recorded that the rebels had been defeated at Pittsburgh Landing in the horrific Battle of Shiloh. Christian likewise remained interested in the news coming from the Eastern Theater and the impact of the war on his family back in Ohio. The Isely family did not share Christian's unbridled passion for the Northern cause. Perhaps because of his family's varying opinions on the war, Christian kept up an especial correspondence with his youngest brother, Henry. Christian wrote that it was his patriotic duty to serve in the defense of his country. This encouragement and dialogue proved to be important; Henry heeded at least part of his brother's continual advice. In late May, Henry wrote a letter from the Berlin Institute in Holmes County, Ohio, informing Christian that he had no desire to debate politics. "If I do write you about politics then we can not agree for ex. last fall I wrote something about the politic of Fremont and I noticed that you looked at the matter just from the opposite." Henry observed that the brothers could not agree on religion or social matters either, but he concluded with an admonishment to be mindful that "there is a warm heart striking for you both in the far east."[71]

On May 29, 1862, Christian penned a letter to his cousins, John F. and Willie Ozenberger, explaining some of his duties and concerns. Christian discussed the amount of lawlessness and bushwhacking going on along the border. He cautioned his cousins, "Don't venture yourself to far, and don't let those infernal rebels & unprincipled bushwhackers surprise you or elude you…. It would make me very sad if such maladies would befall you as did to poor dear Adolph." At the same time that Christian was concerned about his friends and family, he wrote that the spring had been difficult on him.[72]

As the month of June ebbed away, the birth of the Isely baby drew near. Since Elise remained at the home of the Joss family, Christian was able to visit when off duty. During the early morning hours of June 29, Christian recorded, "Last night at 12 o'clock or a little after, My darling Wife gave birth to the first child, a sweet little Boy. God bless both him and his dear Mother who brought him with heart renting pains. This day dawned beautifully upon the newborn." A few days later, Christian wrote, "My dear Love Eliza's [health] still keeps improving. It makes my happiness unbounded. I believe I never felt so happy before. Thanks be to God." As the next few days progressed, Christian had to perform the double duty of being a soldier and a new father. One of his wards died on July 5, and Christian recorded that he was the first to die in his care. A few days later, Christian reported that he was doing his duty at the hospital while running down to the Joss home five times to assist Elise, who was still feeling quite weak. Finally, on July 8, Christian wrote, "Thanks be to God the health of my Wife is improving…. The Child seems to fare better too, but is very noisy."[73]

The fall of 1862 brought hot weather and much excitement to the soldiers and citizens of Leavenworth. In early August, Christian recorded that it was "rumored that 1700 rebels were at Platte City and that they took 30 of our men prisoners. A large force went over from here." On August 5, proof came that Confederates were in the vicinity. "A wounded secesh prisoner was brought into the Hospital pretending to be very much hurt. But after his wound was dressed and as soon as it got dark, he slipt off for the brush." The alarm around the fort increased, for on the following day, Christian wrote that every man who was able to walk left the hospital in search of the "skedaddled secesh" prisoner, without any success.[74]

An even greater concern to Christian was the fact that Elise was ill with an infection. Elise's illness increased her need for help and friends, and she returned with the baby to their cottage in St. Joseph. Her departure and their separation occurred on August 22, 1862, when with the help of the Joss family she returned home. The separation forced both Christian and Elise to carry on their lives, maintaining an undying faith and hope that they would one day be reunited and be given the chance to live the life they had dreamed about when they had courted each other only two short years earlier.

CHAPTER 5

"THIS IS THE HARDEST TASK I EVER FULFILLED"

C hristian recorded in his diary the loneliness that he felt as Elise returned to St. Joseph with their baby. After seeing them off in late August, he wrote, "I presume my dear Wife with darling babe is at home by this time. God grant that they are, and always may be—I came to the Fort yesterday." He worried immensely about his wife and child and often described the reception of a letter as a tonic better than medicine. Elise wrote to Christian, on August 23, that baby Adolph cried quite a bit during the journey. "Everything went pretty well till we had been awhile on the cars. The baby had the cholic so bad so that the poor little thing cryed and would not be comforted, and then I took so sick that I allmost fainted." Elise did not describe what had made her feel ill, only that some kind people on the train helped her and that she was recovering, although a bit weak still.[75]

With Elise's return to St. Joseph, Christian and Elise resumed a correspondence that continued for more than two years. These letters give a detailed account of the thoughts, motivations and passions that they experienced; their marital relationship was completely exposed. These writings are of importance for several reasons. First, since Christian was an enlisted man who never rose above the rank of corporal, he gives an insightful look into the life of the common soldier. He demonstrates that a soldier's life belongs not to him, but to the army in which he serves. Secondly, these letters are of importance because they present an idea of what life was like on the "western frontier." There are seemingly countless diaries and letters of Civil War soldiers who fought in the East, but less numerous are the personal accounts of soldiers who served in the Western Theater, and especially rare are the writings of a Kansas soldier. Lastly, these letters are important because they are by both husband and wife. The soldier's life is exposed as well as that of the civilian spouse. Elise's letters describe the trials of carrying on emotionally and financially while a loved one is gone from home. Through this correspondence, the ideological struggle that is fought at home and on the battlefield is displayed.

On September 3, 1862, Christian wrote a letter of instruction to Elise expressing his desire to improve their station in life. "I am not content to remain in the same place always. I want to advance—to improve. I am not content with the Christian that remains at the same point for years." Christian added that if they survived the terrible contest, we shall "meet once more on earth to live together and find each other so improved both in piety and intelect, that is also in worldly affairs such as habits, manners, education." He concluded by stating that in his rank as corporal he received respect, which made life much easier for him around the fort. He assured Elise that although some of the new recruits were rough characters, most were stout and well-behaved men.[76]

That same evening, Christian penned another letter to his wife. In it, he reported the possibility that he would soon get marching orders and that morale around the fort was quite good. "In the afternoon, we fired 34 rounds from our big siege guns which we have mounted on the banks of the Missouri River. You better believe it made things howl over in Missouri. I guess it made Bushwhackers skeedaddle." Christian remarked that the previous day, rumors had circulated that they would be on the move. "There was a prospect to go to Independence and have a fight with the secesh and probably burn up the town." The detachment consisted of two companies of infantry, one of cavalry and a six-piece light brass artillery unit. Christian cautioned Elise not to be alarmed "if you do not get an answer always so soon for we are liable to be called out any moment, and I do not want to hang back for I would always be ashamed to act so cowardly."[77]

The next few communications between Christian and Elise dealt primarily with their son, referred to in their letters sometimes with the nickname "Sonny." On September 7, 1862, Elise wrote, "Our darling sonny is such a good companion that I sometimes forget you as well as myself. He keeps me pretty busy all the time." Elise expressed her concern about their son's baptism because a neighbor warned her that a "child may get sick and die in a short time and then it grieves the parents so much more" if they have not been baptized. To add to her worries, Reverend Fackler was often gone for periods of time, and it was rumored that he might be leaving St. Joseph for good. Elise sought her husband's guidance. "Now my dear Christian, write me what you think about it and if you think proper. Write me how you want sonny named besides Adolph. The poor little dear has improved so much since I am here. He is so lively and he laughs sweetly so…that he gives me much pleasure."[78]

On September 9, Christian responded. "But darling Eliza it made me quite sad to learn that dear brother Fackler is going to leave St. Joseph—the place where he labored so faithful." Christian then shared that he felt "closely and fraternally attached to him. I hope therefore Eliza that you will go and see him soon and speak to him." The weight of the Civil War and its splitting of the congregation of the Sixth Avenue Presbyterian Church was troubling to the reverend, as well as to Christian. As to baby Adolph and Elise, Christian agreed with Elise that the baptism be performed as soon as possible and requested that he be named "Adolph V[i]ctor McClellan. Eliza dear do not think that I am foolish if I want sonny called after that great General…if you live you will see the time yet, that if our country is saved at all it will be done through that young much abused, but nevertheless, gallant Officer." Christian criticized those who disparaged General George McClellan. "They have added so much to our countries disaster by denouncing the only man in whom all good men place their confidence. His name deserves to be kept in remembrance by all true patriots, therefore I want sonnie called McCLELLAN and also baptized as soon as you like darling." Christian concluded by telling Elise that some of their men chased after the infamous Missouri guerrilla William Quantrill. Quantrill did not fight conventionally. As the Confederate army in Missouri receded south and many soldiers, fed up with the conflict, went home, a few of the more active Southerners left the army and followed the leadership of Quantrill. Quantrill's aim was to take the war to the untouched communities of Kansas, which he did to perfection throughout the first two years of the war.[79]

Christian enclosed two newspaper clippings in his letter to Elise. One short notice dealt with General George McClellan, who had recently resumed command of the Army of the Potomac. The other article related to Colonel Cloud and the 2nd Kansas Volunteer Cavalry. Christian was getting very anxious to be reunited with his unit. Cloud and the men of the 2nd Kansas had engaged some "secesh" at Taborsville, at the crossing of the Neosho River. The skirmish consisted of a running action in which some Confederates surrendered from sheer exhaustion. According to the clipping, Colonel Cloud's command suffered only five wounded, while the

Colonel William F. Cloud, 2nd Kansas Volunteer Cavalry. *Courtesy Kansas State Historical Society.*

Confederates lost about ten killed and many more wounded. The story concluded with the rebels galloping south and Colonel Cloud declaring that the fight demonstrated that rebels should not take to the brush. "The Second is a live regiment and has a live man for a Colonel."[80]

On September 11, 1862, Reverend Fackler replied to Christian's letter. Fackler stated that his concerns as a minister were not the same as those of a layman. "As a minister of Christ, my chief business in this world, is with the perishing souls of my fellowmen. I am more & more convinced every day, that there is little worth living for in this world. I have never felt that ministers of the Gospel ought to join in the strifes & angry contentions of these times." Fackler, in addition to being their minister, was a good friend of Christian and Elise and had much to do with Christian's dedication to Christ. Fackler shared his deep devotion to his friend. "My religion is <u>love</u>, it was the religion of Christ—it is the religion of all good men…I wish to go on in my work, just as I have always done, preaching 'Christ & him crucified' as the only way of life & salvation." Regarding the baptism of Sonny, Fackler concluded by stating that "I will try to see your wife to-morrow."[81]

Elise replied to Christian on September 12. She noted that "the times seem to be very gloomy at present and the people around here are downcast and discouraged." Elise remarked that the Germans especially have "lost all hope and trust in God or man." On a more hopeful note, she informed Christian that Sonny's baptism would take place the Sunday after next. Christian responded just a few days later. He acknowledged that the North was guilty of sins as well, most notably the sin of pride. "We were prone to think that with us success cannot be an impossibility." Christian stated that the Northerners have been proud and boastful, thinking that they could easily punish the South. They have made money their God, according to Christian, but finally, "They begin to feel the horrors of War. It brings them to their senses." Union supporters have been humbled, but "with an eye looking to God for help we will soon be able to make traitors respect our dear with blood purchased Government and gladden the patriots heart. The Government will only be much dearer to all but it will be much stronger."

He concluded by stating that a recent military expedition reported that Quantrill was ransacking Olathe, Kansas. The report was correct. Quantrill, in retribution for the execution of one of his men, raided the town of Olathe. As Quantrill and his 140 guerrillas made their way to Olathe, they stopped along the way at various farms and homesteads where they knew Union sympathizers lived and shot them. As Quantrill began his raid, he promised to kill ten men as a payback. He killed ten before he even reached the town. Once in Olathe, Quantrill and his men killed three recently enlisted soldiers and a member of a militia unit. Quantrill promised the rest of the soldiers and civilians that if they did not resist, no one else would be killed. Three civilians objected, and they were killed. The rest were paroled the following day after the guerrillas completed their theft and plunder of the town. Quantrill and his men departed for Missouri the next day, but the entire episode drove Union sympathizers to a more intense hatred of Quantrill and his band.[82]

In a letter to Christian dated September 19, Elise discussed Reverend Fackler, baptism and the naming of the baby. Fackler advised Elise that they should drop the name Victor, a suggestion Christian consented to in a future letter. Elise then described baby Adolph. "Sonny is quite a smart fellow, only he is a little cross day time so that I cannot even go to church."

Elise remarked that if he awoke and she was not right there, he almost cried himself to death. No one could quiet him with all of his or her efforts. He weighed eleven pounds, and "everybody says he favors his father exactly."[83]

Christian's next few letters dealt with the situation around Fort Leavenworth. Since being attached to a battery, he noticed that the men were not drilled properly in artillery tactics. Also, while all of the good men were assigned to their respective regiments, "the mean ones remain, such as a lot of drunken Irish whelps belonging to the 1st & 7th Kansas." According to Christian, such soldiers were heroic talkers and used vulgar language, but they did no good for anyone. As to Christian's duties, he was commanded to drill some men, a duty that did not come easily to him. Recently, a parade was held. "It was a brilliant affair, to see all the companies in their dress uniforms." Most of the fort's garrison consisted of the 8th Kansas Infantry and the 3rd Wisconsin Cavalry. The men of the 7th Kansas rode out only a few days before the dress parade. Christian added that he was terribly lonesome. However, he encouraged Elise to put their trust in God, and soon a "brilliant Sun" would emerge and bring forth a splendor.

As the end of September approached, Christian received a new uniform and had the opportunity to hear General James Lane speak. Christian also received a canteen, one pair of knit drawers and an undershirt. These supplies were a welcome sight to the soldier, and he teasingly asked Elise, "Would you not like to see me in Artillery Uniform Dear?" As to General Lane's speech, he warned the soldiers to be honest and avoid alcohol. Most especially, he encouraged them to avoid the Leavenworth grog shops. Christian further noted that some men of the 11th Kansas arrived. They were good men, but he noticed that near them several women and children were living in tents. They were obviously quite poor, and Christian felt sorry for them. Lastly, Christian recalled a remark that Elise had made, referring to the Civil War as an unholy one. "Now how can you express yourself in that manner if you consider our cause a just one? No indeed my Darling as a loyal woman you must not term this war an unholy one as long as we are struggling for right, justice and liberty, but the rebellion is unjust and unholy."[84]

As Christian penned his letter of September 30, 1862, tragedy was about to strike the Isely family. As with most personal news of the day, the information came in a letter. Elise wrote on October 5, with a heart full of grief, "I take the pen in hand to state to you what happened in this short space of time. My pet, our darling took his departure from a world of sorrows to one of bliss. Yes, my beloved Christian, our darling sonny is no more. He died. He died last Friday night. The will of the lord be done." The baby had not been sick, only at times fretful and crying, which everyone described as colic. "So Friday night, I went to bed little thinking what would happen before morning. He nursed after I went to bed with him and as I think we both fell asleep." Elise awoke a little after 1:00 a.m., and when she felt for the baby, he was a corpse. "Nothing could be done to restore him to life. He was dead. Now dear Christian, you are again the only one left to me."

Elise's brother, Fred, proceeded to take care of all the details, as he had after the death of the baby's namesake, Elise's brother Adolph. As a soldier's son, Adolph's coffin would be paid for, but Elise and Fred decided to buy a nicer casket. Elise then wrote that the baby was buried the day before in the "graveyard on the hill where you used to go so often to pour out your heart in prayer before God." Elise revealed another heartache: the baby had not been baptized. Brother Fackler had not arrived as promised, having been called away by duty. Elise comforted Christian by stating, "Dear Christian, you may rest assured that our sonny was well taken care of in his short life." Fred had consulted a doctor the morning after the baby died, and based on the baby's age and lack of symptoms, the doctor believed that the baby had died of a disease of the heart. She also assured Christian that the baby did not suffer, but only fell asleep and never awakened. "Now dearest, do not grieve yourself for mine and your own sake until you get sick. But be firm as a Christian should be and remember our darling has escaped a world of troubles." Elise concluded with a poignant remark. "This is the hardest task I ever fulfilled." Their baby was only three months and seven days old.[85]

On October 6, 1862, Christian recorded in his diary that he had received the news of his son's death. "Today I felt a kind of sadness without knowing why. In the evening, I received a letter from my darling Wife stating to my inexpressable grief that our Darling Sonny is no more." In the days to come, Christian wondered why it had pleased God to take "our dear innocent babe from us." Finally, he became resigned that God meant all of this for some purpose. His letter to Elise written on October 9 expressed the deep sorrow. "O can it be possible that our Darling Sonny is no more? I could hardly believe the statement at its first reading. But alas I am obliged to believe it—obliged to believe that our only, our first Child is dead and buried, without its father even knowing that it was sick." Christian, who had not seen his son for a few months, then lamented, "O is it posible that I am to see my dear babes innocent face no more while on earth?" He was "sad to say that I did not even give it a last kiss." Christian was convinced that the tragedy would make both he and Elise better disciples of God, "that we may be better fitted to be his meek and humble followers, and better instruments in His hands to do something for His honor and glory and the salvation of mankind." Perhaps to provide a diversion, Christian suggested that this was an excellent time for Elise to return to school to improve herself. Christian closed with a postscript discussing his first anniversary of military service. While God has been, in Christian's words, quite merciful, "he has sorely wounded my heart by taking away two dear beings that were grown so close to my heart, yet I have no doubt that it is all well as the Lord has willed it."[86]

Naturally, the next few letters that passed between the Iselys were filled with mentions of the loss of their infant son. In an attempt to console each other, they asked the nagging questions of why this terrible tragedy occurred. Christian continued to urge Elise to attend school. Elise seemed to be less than convinced. Christian argued that it was the ideal time for her to attend school for her betterment. He truly wanted her to improve her education. Moreover, he was also hoping to get her involved in something that would take her mind off the loss of their baby. Both Christian and Elise urged each other not to sink into depression. On October 17, Elise wrote Christian from Willow Dale, Kansas, "I avail myself of the first opportunity to write you a few lines and to let you know how I am getting along since it has pleased the Lord to take our little darling from us…. My love, let us not be down cast, and in all let us give thanks and praise to God who doeth all things well. It was our little dear's gain and maybe he has a mission to perform in yon world of bliss, and besides he is not lost to us." Elise reflected that their "sweet little Angel" was in heaven, and although "he cannot come to us, we will go to him."[87]

Before Adolph died, both Christian and Elise wanted to have the baby baptized. For various reasons, this was not done. Reverend Fackler wrote an apologetic letter to Christian on October 18. "Not only did I feel sad on account of the loss, that you & your poor wife had met with, but it made me doubly sad, to think that I was absent from home when the dear child died. If I had been here, I could have at least offered sympathy & condolence to your wife, in her great bereavement & loneliness." Fackler tried to console Christian by explaining that the baby was no longer in a world of pain. "Heaven now has for your both, an additional attraction. You may always think of that place, as the blessed home of your child…We may not be able to see it now, but after a while, in the light of eternity, it will all be made clear & plain."[88]

Elise composed a poem for Adolph, written on the back of a letter sent by Christian that is undated. It is possible that Elise sent the poem along with an earlier letter:

"This Is the Hardest Task I Ever Fulfilled"

POEM FOR BABY ADOLPH (B. JUNE 28, 1862–D. OCT. 5, 1862)

Though sad with grief, yet time rolled on,
June filled my heart with happiness,
By giving me a darling Son;
Thus turning grief once more to bliss.
His months however were but few
His life—was but a hasty stay
He took his flight away from view,
To shine in his immortal ray.
On one sad October night—
My heart seemed to break with pain—
Dear babe was snatched from mortal sight.
To see it live was hope in vain.
One friend is left most dear of all
It is my husband far away
What Oh! If he yet too should fall
O God have pitty when I pray, hear me pray.
O spare him mercy that dear life
O that my dear remaining friend
That I may be his happy Wife
When war has closed—expelled each fiend
Be calm my child, I hear thy pleas
Thy husband at a rolling brook
In supplication bends his knees
Be firm! and read the sacred Book.[89]

Christian penned a letter on October 22 to Elise. For the first time, in some detail, he shared the feelings of his family back in Ohio. Apparently, he received communications from his family in the preceding months. The only letters from the family in Ohio that exist are primarily from Christian's youngest brother, Henry. It is possible that Henry wrote Christian more often, but at least a few letters written by Christian's parents and sisters are absent from the collection. Regardless, Christian, who was never quiet about his feelings, shared with Elise his opinions regarding the news from Ohio. "I received a very sad letter from my Sister Ann...yesterday according to it there exists an awful state of things in Ohio now." Both of Christian's brothers, Henry and Fred, were drafted, largely against their will. Christian's mother placed the blame for their situation at the feet of the abolitionists. "My sister has written me a very bitter letter…. She thinks I express sentiments direct in opposition to the teachings of the Bible because I expressed myself unfriendly to slavery. Poor sister, I pity her and all the rest of them." After reading her angry letter, Christian went to the woods and shed tears on behalf of his entire family. He prayed and forgave them. Christian explained, "They are nearly all Democrats where they live and opposed to the war in the Township where they live—a piece of land 6 miles square—47 have to be drafted. That shows how poorly they turned out in volunteering." As a resident of the border, Christian had a difficult time understanding people who were indifferent to the war. He found the indifference expressed by some Northerners to be as damaging as the rebellion itself.[90]

The Isely letters of late October and early November share a few themes. One is Christian's continuing desire to have Elise attend school. Although he hoped to persuade her, "I will not dictate for you. I will only give you my advice and opinion, which you can either accept or reject. It is my sole desire to make you happy. I married you for that purpose, though I have not as yet accomplished it." A second theme echoed by both Christian and Elise was their shared consolation over the loss of their baby. These letters are more genuinely affectionate than earlier letters. Christian, for example, wrote on November 9, "I love your dear letters like a sweet little idol." He "fancied my darling Eliza at my side and close to my heart." Christian concluded with, "Yours till death in love…. If I could again meet, My Darling and see her face—To kiss her would be sweet, With a warm affectiate embrace." These are very animated and heartfelt sentiments, even for Christian, who was always an expressive writer.[91]

Another growing concern of Christian's was his disagreement with his family members. The fact that Henry Isely might soon be on a battlefield obviously heightened everyone's attention. The letters show that Christian was a bit of an outsider among his family. His opinions may have been shared by a fair number of Northerners and men with whom he served, but they were not embraced by members of the Isely family in Ohio.

Chapter 6

"THESE WOUNDS WILL REMAIN"

As 1862 came to a close, the Isely family disagreements with Christian became more apparent. Christian informed Elise in early November about a hateful letter his sister sent. She wrote that "the Niggers will have to take you and our Babe if I get killed in this war, because I am so willing to fight for them and sacrifice myself for them." His sister stated that blacks were rejoicing "when they hear that so many white men are falling. It being a good prospect for them to get white Wives." Christian replied that she need not trouble herself about Elise because she had a "kind Father...he would not let you be in want for any thing—and as for the child, the Lord has provided for him and has taken him to Himself." Christian turned to Elise for support and consolation. "We have married each other to make each other happy if we can and bear each other's burdens." Christian emphasized that they should keep nothing from each other, whether good or bad. "If I could again my Darling meet, And see her face, To kiss her would be more than sweet, And warm embrace."[92]

One interesting diary entry written about this same time concerned the various feelings of soldiers who were stationed at Fort Leavenworth. Of course, not all Northern soldiers were as adamant about preserving the Union as was Christian. For various reasons, many thought that the Confederacy should be allowed to exist as a separate nation. Some were lukewarm toward ending slavery. Others thought it was not worth getting killed. And still others believed that slavery would never be totally extracted from the Southern way of life. Christian mentioned that the soldiers at Fort Leavenworth had formed a discussion group. On December 3, the question of that day was whether or not the Southern Confederacy was entitled to its independence. After some debate, a vote was taken on the matter, and the affirmative won. Christian noted at the end of this entry, "I was on the neg[ative]." Christian and Elise's antipathy toward slavery was apparent in many of the letters.[93]

Christian had been a Douglas Democrat in 1860, but by the end of 1862 and early 1863, it was apparent that he was shifting politically. Although it would take some time before Christian claimed to be a Republican, he dismissed his Ohio relatives with the comment that "they are all Democrats." By 1863, two events exacerbated the situation: the Emancipation Proclamation and the Union military draft. Now the war seemed to have one overriding goal, emancipating the slaves, and Christian's Copperhead relatives were subjected to being drafted to fight in a cause they did not support. Copperheads began to protest in earnest, and the eventual Democratic presidential candidate of 1864, George B. McClellan, was viewed by some as a tool of the Copperheads. Antiwar rhetoric increased during the campaign, with Copperheads arguing that the destruction of the Union was caused by abolitionists. Other opponents of the conflict were more emphatic, simply stating that they would not fight to free blacks.[94]

Christian was concerned with the political and moral ramifications of the Civil War. He intimated in a few of his letters that the term "abolitionist" made him uncomfortable. He was very much against slavery, but abolitionists were portrayed as radicals, and he resisted that label. As the war progressed and Christian embraced Lincoln and the Republican cause, both he and Elise remarked that if their belief system was that of the abolitionists, then that was what they should be called. Obviously, this put him at odds with most members of his Ohio family, a thread woven throughout much of their remaining correspondence.

In late November 1862, Christian received a letter from Henry, a member of the 67th Ohio Volunteer Infantry, Company C. Henry detailed his journey from home to Suffolk, Virginia, and the scene of battle. Many of the men in Henry's unit were from Winesburg and mutual friends of Christian. Henry observed, "It is a very nice country here, but it is all devastated. The fences are all gone, and the forests cut down; the Sentiments of the citizens is secesh all-together; we are fortified by breastworks. There are about 16,000 men here." Henry and Christian shared a martial bond with each other. Although their politics plainly differed, they were both soldiers fighting for the Northern cause. Other than Elise, Christian wrote and received more letters from Henry than any other member of his family.[95]

On November 17, Christian shared with Elise some personal thoughts. He received a touching letter from his mother, her sadness increased now because two of her sons were in the service. He also received a letter from Henry, and while the tone was truly patriotic, it was also "unrelenting democratic and down on abolitionist[s]." Apparently both of Christian's brothers, Henry and Fred, were drafted, but at some point, for reasons not clearly stated, they were released and given the option to volunteer. Henry chose to volunteer with many of the other Winesburg boys, while

Henry Isely, circa 1863. *Courtesy Isely family, from Sunbonnet Days.*

Fred did not. Christian also wrote that he heard from his regiment; it engaged the enemy in Arkansas, and one man in his company was killed. The regiment was currently camped 150 miles below Fort Scott, and "I am hoping to try my best to get there or else the first thing I know the war is over and I have not done the first thing for my dear Land and Country." In a postscript, Christian added "a few private remarks. In the first place I do not wish that you should make yourself very familiar with secesh acquaintance[s]." Christian mentioned two neighbor ladies in particular, including a woman named Mrs. Lillie. "I want you to keep away from her house. Giving aid and sympathy to rebels is played out." Christian also remarked that the food at the fort was not fit for a dog to eat. Still, he maintained that his spirits were high and that he had many "a good chance to go out for secret prayer, there is so much timber and brush around here where I can spend many rich seasons." Moreover, while many Northerners suffered, Christian maintained that Southerners trying to remain loyal to the Union were suffering the most.[96]

The next few letters by Elise revealed that she remained a bit depressed and gloomy and missed Christian and the baby. She was also looking forward to going to school for a three-month term. On one occasion, she heard cannons booming around St. Joseph and wondered what it meant. She was also disturbed by the news that General McClellan had been removed, for the second time, following the Battle of Antietam. "I am indeed very sorry if only half of what is said about him is true." Elise had not realized how much faith she had put in McClellan until then. "I feel just as if a dear friend had become untrue." Christian replied with a cheering letter written in early December. In a romantic mood, Christian described Elise as "the object of the sweetest reflection and tenderest affection, of things earthly. And without you my Dear, it seems to me that this world would be an empty unfriendly desert." Christian felt "happy and exceedingly cheerful, though I am placed far from you…yet I am continually made happy when I remember that there is such a being as my dear Eliza. A being given to me and preserved for me by a merciful God." Christian still hoped to get a furlough but warned Elise not to get her hopes up, "for there is nothing more uncertain than a soldier's promise."[97]

Illness was certainly on Elise's mind in the last few months of 1862. She originally said that one of the reasons she wanted to spend time at her parent's home was because of her mother's ailments. In a letter dated December 9, Elise wrote that her father's health was consistently failing and that her brother Fred was so sick "that we all thought he would die. He all at once became helpless and his breath became shorter every minute and if it had lasted a little longer getting worse, I have no doubt he could not have held out." Elise stated that while Fred was not at all well yet, he was improving. She also confessed that she had not informed Christian how ill Fred really was because he already "had enough to bear then and I do not write it now to put you in tro[u]ble but you told I should keep nothing from you be it well or woe."[98]

On Christmas Day, a lonely but a thankful Elise wrote to Christian of her thoughts about the preceding year. "Christmas, has at last come; and I have lived in the fond hope of spending it in your dear company; but my hopes, have been frustrated. I looked for your coming in vain; and have made up my mind to be content without you." Even though the day was overcast with heavy clouds, Elise stated that the gloom had no effect on her mind. "The Lord has, in mercy spared both of us; thus far, for in the present time, there is many a wounded and almost broken heart; and many a family without a home, and God in mercy has so kindly, blessed us with friends and home…I am blessed above asking, and understanding." Elise added that their lives would improve, if not on earth then in the eternal, "where trials, tribulations, sickness, and grief and our last enemy death shall have no right over us. There we shall ever be happy." Christian similarly jotted down in his diary thoughts about the previous year. The terrible scenes that ravaged the nation were disheartening at times, and although the "scenes have passed…it is not so with the memory of these scenes. They cause many a heart to bleed as if though the wound has been inflicted but yesterday. And these wounds will remain new for a long time to come. The past year has indeed been a dark and sad one." Christian also expressed concern for President Lincoln, but "thank God, he stood firm as a rock." As for Christian's devotion, "My all is at present devoted for my Country, the Land of Liberty, my thoughts center there." Christian declared that the enemies of truth and liberty would soon be banished, "delivered from danger—from the traitor's hand. O God wilt thou not in mercy interpose speedily and deliver us…that all the true hearts of the country may awake as to their duty, and they may rush to rescue, that land that was left to us as a Legacy by our noble forfathers."[99]

As the new year dawned, President Lincoln's Emancipation Proclamation, stating that all of the slaves in rebellious states were free, went into effect. While Southerners had no intention of complying with Lincoln's proclamation, the document in many ways defined and galvanized the cause of the Union. Some Northerners felt that it would alienate loyal Unionists who cared little for the lot of the slave. Others worried that it could alienate border state citizens whose loyalty was already divided. Regardless, Lincoln, in his role as commander in chief, designed the proclamation to aid the Union war effort, realizing that a constitutional amendment was needed to abolish slavery throughout the United States. Christian joyously recorded in his diary on January 1, 1863, that "universal Emancipation of the Blacks is this day proclaimed throughout the rebellous States. The final doom of the traitors is fixed!" Elise discussed the impact of the Emancipation Proclamation many years later. Some in St. Joseph, such as fellow church member John Colhoun, anticipated the ending of slavery by freeing their slaves in advance. Colhoun, a Pennsylvanian, was married to a woman from Virginia who had inherited some slaves. He never approved of slavery, however, and after he freed his slaves, he eased their entry into society, even helping some to obtain work. One became the janitor of the Presbyterian church. Still, Elise wrote that the news of the Emancipation Proclamation encouraged some blacks to seek freedom in Kansas and Iowa.[100]

In the middle of January, Elise wrote to Christian that, true to their previous discussions, she had made her decision to enter school. "I have been to school today for the first time but I cannot tell you anything much about it untill I have tried a litte longer. I go to that Lady which teaches in the basement of the Baptist church." Elise wrote later that she returned to school, at the suggestion of her husband, in an effort to help her deal with the grief over the loss of Adolph. Elise attended a girls' school, her "classmates being both of Union and Confederate sympathies. They knew that I had a husband in the army, but they also learned that in the company of secessionists I held my tongue, and so we never had any disagreements." The same difficulty faced Elise at church, where, she wrote, "old friends greeted me and talked about their sons and brothers and husbands, some of whom were fighting on side and some on the other." Elise wrote that many congregations split during this time but that Reverend Fackler's kept theirs together "by the power of his personality and devotion to the church."[101]

Christian was quite happy that Elise was attending school. He was always concerned with improvement and good moral conduct. This philosophy is evidenced in much of his writings. Still, of course, bad things happen to good people, and Christian and Elise were no exception. One particular incident occurred at Fort Leavenworth in the second week of January, shortly after pay was issued. "After I had made a turn around a building and walked off about 4 rods, I put my hands in the pockets, and to my great surprise found that my pocket book was gone. The feelings that overcame me were such as cannot be well described." As Christian retraced his steps, he came around a corner and faced two men approaching him. One of them slipped something into his pocket and laughed. Christian was confident that it was his pocketbook in the man's pocket. Both men belonged to the 8th Kansas, and both had been drinking. Christian confronted them. "They first tried to deny it, but I stuck to them in a manner that they seen that they were obliged to give up the money and were convinced that it was mine. At last they agreed to give up the money if I agreed to treat." After Christian informed the men that he did not drink, he decided to give them some small change and told them not to spend it on whiskey. Christian wrote that while he felt sorry that he gave money to whiskey-drinking men, he was relieved he "got off so light."[102]

Although Elise returned to school, she and Christian made plans about what she should do after her three-month term was completed. Letters that Christian received from his family in Ohio convinced him that Elise should pay them an extended visit. Elise had never met any of Christian's relatives, so the trip had an added appeal. Although the visit was months in the future, Christian was full of travel information and advice. "Never move to get out of the cars till the Conductor comes in and sings out the name of the place.

Never pay any attention to loafers or runners. Never venture too far away from the Depot in a strange place." Christian also warned, "Never be to friendly to any body that wishes to be inquisitive or ready to give information and instruction. Be thankful and Lady like to the Conductors and those that assist you. These Rules well followed up will bring my Lady Love safe to my boyhood home, God being her Helper."

Christian's friends and family back in Ohio were obviously on his mind, as they continued to communicate through the mails. One such letter was penned on January 14 at Winesburg by family friend John Kunzli, the father of six young children and an outspoken opponent of slavery. Kunzli confided that he felt politically closer to Christian than to his Democratic brothers, Fred and Henry. A military draft had taken place in which Kunzli, Henry and Fred were all selected. The drafted men were informed that they would be added to the ranks of volunteer regiments, and some immediately began to seek substitutes at sums ranging between $160 and $350. Kunzli, by now concerned with the future of his children, hired a substitute. Fred Isely hired a substitute as well, although his reasons are a little less clear. His stated reason many years later was the care of his aged parents. Henry, however, consented to join willingly, much to the dismay of his entire family. Kunzli concluded by stating that he was glad he had lived to see the president declare "the poor bondsmen of the rebels free."[103]

Christian had anticipated for quite some time that he would be ordered away from Fort Leavenworth. Rumors abounded in the first two weeks of January that his battery or the men on detached duty would be reunited with their regiments at Fort Scott. Christian found out on January 14 that the rumors were false. Still, spirits were high, as Fort Leavenworth had a high-ranking visitor, Major General James Blunt. Blunt commanded the Department of Kansas until the summer of 1863, when he took the field as the commander of the Army of the Frontier. He was escorted into the fort by four infantry and four cavalry companies. "We placed the Cannons on the levee and fired him a grand Salute." As to the rumors of movement, Christian wrote that while they were ready to go, "nothing further is now known whether any of us go down south or not."[104]

Christian desperately wanted to change duty posts. True, as long as he was stationed at Fort Leavenworth, he was probably safe from battle. But he also knew that he had to remain in the army for his full term of three years. Not being able to see Elise often, and with an obvious patriotic zeal, Christian wanted to get in the fight. He commented on a few occasions that he feared the war would end before he performed the soldierly duties of fighting in the field. He did not want to be thought of as a coward or an evader of his duties. Another frustration for Christian was the sort of individuals who often came to the fort. He described many of these as hangers-on, drinkers and shirkers. He had grown tired of their presence, and according to his letters and diaries, it could certainly be deduced that he was capable of conveying to them their shortcomings or sins.

Tired of the tedious garrison duty, Christian turned to self-improvement, just as Elise returned to school. Christian wrote that he was reading a great deal, including the fourth volume of *History of the Reformation*. In late January, Elise shared her own thoughts about mutual improvement. "I have taken up another study to day and that is Ancient History." Elise wrote that it would give her knowledge in many ways and especially of the Bible. She also studied arithmetic, grammar and geography. Elise occasionally sent Christian original writing, including one entitled, "The Contrast between Happiness and Misery," a short story concerning the differences between two households. In the caring family, children obeyed their parents out of love, not fear. "But you might ask what makes them so happy? Religion. Vice is at the root of misery. Virtue is at the beginning of all that is good."[105]

War often compels combatants and their families to do much soul searching. The Civil War saw many salvations, rededications and moments of spiritual renewal. This awakening of religious fervor occurred on the battlefield and on the homefront. Elise related on many occasions that the spirit of revival was prevalent in St. Joseph. Elise's letter of January 31, 1863, stated that "about 20 persons have again united with our church this week…. The Baptists have had and are still having a great revival and so has our church…thanks be to God, he is on our side and if he is for us, who will be against us." Elise informed Christian that "I had my likeness taken this week and I saw brother Fackler's there to sell, and I purchased it for you. I thought you would like it." Christian received the photographs a few days later, noting that it was one of the happiest moments in his life to receive his wife's likeness. Elise closed by admonishing Christian to "not give yourself too much to politics, think of your higher calling, for I really believe we have come to a strange period of time and God is working wonders in the hearts of men."[106]

Naturally, as the war progressed Christian spoke more of his political leanings. Elise, in contrast, wrote sparingly of politics. One diary entry of Christian's, on January 31, expresses a forceful political opinion. "If our dear Land and Country will have to fall, it will not be on account of the southern army, but on account of northern traitors that call themselves Democrats."

It is an interesting comment in light of the fact that Christian started the war as a self-confessed Douglas Democrat.[107]

On February 9, Christian wrote of a new bunkmate named John Hendry. His previous bunkmate was Sergeant Gill, a pretentious hypocrite who acted treacherously against Christian. Hendry, a blessed contrast, read the Bible often and belonged to the Baptist church in St. Joseph. "He is a whole souled unionist, a lover of his country and true worker for, & lover of the cause of Christ. He don't make much show and is quite unpretensive." Christian often read aloud Elise's "dear letters in which he takes no small interest" in the news from St. Joseph. Speaking of her letters, Christian urged Elise to abandon the habit of writing up and down in the margins of her letters and added, "I do not think Eliza dear that there is a word in the english language as you write 'awail' but rather 'avail.' But Dear I will not criticise your letters for I am well aware that they contain no more faults than mine; the word 'awail' however appears several times and I make the correction by your kind request." He concluded by stating that while he hoped for a chance to work in the post carpenter shop at the fort, it appeared the opportunity would not come to pass.[108]

In a letter written on February 18, Christian made no mention of stylistic or grammatical faults. "I had the pleasure yesterday to receive my own Love's Letter which is full of burning affection, tender Love and spiritual Life. O Eliza! My own dear sweet Eliza what would I do without you, in this often so unfriendly world; it seems to me that I could not endure to live without you." A week later, Christian told Elise of mail he received from his family, enclosing brother Henry's likeness. One of the letters, penned by Christian's mother, expressively "stated that my letters and Henry's do her a great deal of good and went to show that she—God bless her kind, motherly heart—that she thinks not a little of her two sons in the army; and by the way also of my gentle Eliza. She also stated that she would like it very much if you would come to them this Spring. What say you to this my Love?" Christian was not optimistic about visiting St. Joseph on leave but sent Elise some valentines. Christian also added that he had written her some poetry and that the detachment at the fort fired thirty-four rounds from the big siege guns in honor of George Washington's birthday.[109]

Christian during this period wrote an article denouncing slavery. He based his argument on scripture. Nowhere in the Bible does it state that one man should eat the bread of another one, Christian claimed. In fact, God told Adam that "in the sweat of thy face, shall thou eat bread." Christian contended that as the centuries passed, people became increasingly sinful.

Such was the case with slavery; it grew with time, to the point of becoming customary in some societies. As to the argument that slavery is acceptable because it is mentioned in the Bible, Christian noted that polygamy is mentioned as well but not condoned. If the United States were to be a truly Christian nation, it must become "free from every scheme of bondage…. O sons and daughters of America, let it be a shining light to other nations." Christian cited nineteen biblical passages that expressly denounced the ideas of slavery. Christian stated that these scriptures taught a number of lessons, including the equality of all men, just compensation for labor and giving freed slaves justice and equality when possible. Christian concluded, "Now with all these and many other proves [proofs] against them, how can any one charge the Bible as being for <u>slavery</u>?!"[110]

In a letter dated March 3, Christian explained to Elise the criticisms heaped on him from within his own family. Brother-in-law J.G. Abele, for example, "wounded my feelings…in regard to my political views and my religious views." Christian maintained that he never mentioned politics to his relatives, yet those "northern half-traitors and easy-going patriots" always attacked him. Abele, a minister, apparently urged Christian to refrain from discussing politics. "But as long as a rebel or sympathizer is found," Christian pledged to Elise, "I will oppose him more so hereafter than heretofore, because if I don't do it they will assail me any way, and think me already conquered." Christian added, "Such is the spirit of treason all over the land, and I love to despise that spirit…. I begin to think more and more that it may become your duty to go to Ohio sometime this spring." Christian defiantly added, in regard to his enemies, "What does it matter: my body they can kill, but my soul they cannot."[111]

The next letter that came from Christian turned out to be his last for a few weeks, for a good reason. In a letter dated March 8, 1863, Christian discussed the well-being of his cousins, Freddie and Willie. The 5th Kansas Cavalry had recently been in Mississippi, but the men were now back in Kansas. Four days later, Christian was granted a leave. It was the first chance Christian and Elise had to be reunited since before the death of baby Adolph. Christian wrote in his diary on March 12, "I got a pass this morning to pay my dear Wife a visit. I went to Weston and there took the cars to St. Joseph where I arrived safe in the evening." The next few diary entries express Christian's happiness and hopefulness. He "enjoyed my meeting with my dear sweet little Wife very much. She gave me such a warm tender and affectionate reception. God bless her." St. Joseph itself was pretty much "the same old place still. I was only sad to see so many secesh faces. But my dear Eliza makes me happy and our dear church edified me." On Sunday, March 15, the Iselys had "a blessed time in our dear church. O glad I was to hear Bro. Fackler once more." Christian enjoyed his "visit so much. It is such a blessed thing to be married to a loving Wife…. The good work in our dear church is still progressing. God be praised."[112]

Christian's diary entry of March 18 mentioned for the first time his deceased child. "The sky was cloudy, I went to my darling sonnie's grave to heighten the sunken mound. His dear soul is in heaven, and at rest." The following day, Christian and Elise traveled to her father's home near Willow Dale, "the place where my dear Eliza and I spent our days of love, that still hover about in our memory." As happy as Christian and Elise were during those few days, the time soon came for him to return to Fort Leavenworth. "This is the last day again for sometime at least, that my darling Wife and I are permited to be together in happiness. God bless, keep and preserve us both." On March 25, Christian "took leave from my precious treasure and Wife, it was again a sad parting. I arrived safe at Fort Leavenworth this evening." Upon his return, Christian "was received very affectionately by all the boys, but I felt painfully sad. This was a beautiful morning, and so I took a ramble for meditation and prayer." Two days later, Christian recorded, "Never grief seemed more painful to me than yesterday. Death cannot be more painful. Today, I feel much better. I got a fine letter from Bro. Henry."[113]

Christian encouraged Elise to write letters to as many soldiers as possible, especially to his brother, Henry. She did, and on March 14, 1863, Henry responded with a letter to Elise from Hilton Head, South Carolina. Thanking her for writing, Henry acknowledged that "although I am personally a stranger to you, I flatter myself with the fact that speaking through the medium of writing, I have an intimate friend and relative in you, therefore to express my gratitude for your well meant, lovely lines." The camp conditions were summed up by Henry: "I take a piece of a crackerbox for a desk upon my knees and answer it [your letter] in my feeble style and manner, which are checked yet by the loud talk and laughters, and the very frequent deep curses of the never satisfying card players, which I deem one of the worst practices of the soldiers." His regiment was reported to be moving toward Charleston soon. "If I should fall before the walls of that City, I hope to God that we will meet in Heaven once, where we shall part no more."[114]

The correspondence between the two Isely brothers, Henry and Christian, continued. Obviously, with both men serving in the military, they had something in common, although they agreed on very little else. Henry continued to be a Democrat, and he often disagreed with Christian's religious observations. Christian had encouraged members of his family to be patriots and defenders of the Union. Henry, although drafted, responded to the call, not buying a substitute or otherwise trying to avoid military service. While Christian seemed to be the most willing to see combat, it was Henry who found himself closer to the face of battle.

CHAPTER 7

"STRICTLY LOYAL AND PURELY 'ANTI SLAVERY'"

In the last week of March, Elise bid farewell once again to Christian as his leave ended and he returned to duty. The transition period proved to be difficult. Elise wrote that after she left Christian at the rail depot, she "felt sad for some time, but I thought it was best to be cheerful and take things easy for we had had such a happy time together…. I then wiped my tears away in the hope that if I should shed tears again so near you they would be tears of joy." Elise added that she was thankful to have a husband as temperate and virtuous as Christian. "We can rest at ease and rest assured that as far as such things are concerned, we are safe." She ended her letter with the familiar theme that if they were to be parted on earth, they had the knowledge of meeting again in "yon Heavenly world of bliss. Where there's no parting and there be forever each others."

Christian's transition was equally difficult. Exchanging the tranquility of home for the noisy, rough life at the fort magnified the differences between civilian and military life. Although the soldiers of the fort welcomed him with brotherly love, he wrote on March 30 that he had bread and coffee for a meal, "for I can't call it supper." He added that it was Elise's love and affection that took his mind off the monotony of soldiering. Christian was optimistic about the cause of the Union, even predicting that "six more months may wind up the whole affair." He claimed that the Southern Confederacy was drifting into monarchy. As to those Northerners who disagreed with the cause of the Union, he told Elise, "I hope you may never be discouraged when you hear copperheads, and faultfinders howl." These Copperheads were enemies of the republic just as Satan and his infidels were the enemies of the kingdom of Christ. In Christian's view, a short stay in Dixie would cure "their sore malady…. I assure you, that if the rebels in their benighted Confederacy, fared as well as those do within the borders of the loyal States, they would almost consider themselves in heaven." Christian ended this letter by stating that all Copperheads were opposed to anything truly loyal and that for his part, he would do anything to preserve "our dear American 'Republic' founded by George Washington,' even it if has to be unto death."[115]

Christian had developed a sincere distaste for Copperheads or anyone who opposed the federal government. While he probably came into contact with these types of people occasionally, the Copperhead sentiment that was most frustrating to him was that of his own family. As with abolitionists, Copperheads came in varying degrees. It can be stated with a fair degree of certainty that Christian had abolitionist sentiments, while most of his family had Copperhead or antiwar leanings. Undoubtedly, Christian's travels, time in the west and exposure to slavery had hastened an evolution in his thinking that was markedly different from his Ohio relatives. The question remains, though: were Christian's parents in opposition to the Union effort because they desperately hoped that the war would end, bringing their sons home, or did the Iselys object to the war based on their political convictions? It would appear that as parents of soldiers they could respond one of two ways. They could either press for and support wholehearted victory and thus bring a quick resolution to the war and their sons' service. Or they could press for the war to be ended immediately without a military resolution to the conflict. Many members of Christian's family chose the latter position, insisting—as many Copperheads did—that this was not their war to fight and that even if slaves should be free, it was not their job to free them. A final motivation came from prior political affiliation. Many of the Copperheads had been Democrats before the war and were intent on remaining in the same camp.

The next few letters between Christian and Elise dealt primarily with the topics of loneliness and religion. Elise wrote that she felt sorry that Christian was so lonely. He expressed his loneliness to Elise, but the strain of disagreement in his own family, along with the personal losses of his young brother-in-law and infant son, were weighing on him. Elise shared with Christian the inscription she wanted on baby Adolph's tombstone: "Ere sin could blight and sorrow fade; Death comes from friendly care; The opening bud to heaven conveyed; And bade it blossom there." She was confident "that all our trials will prove a blessing to us in the end, only let us pray for willing hearts to bear it all patiently." After the discussion of loneliness was played out, Christian turned to a point of theology. He declared that, although many have varying views of the Antichrist, "the Revelation shows plainly that the Pope is the Anti-Christ prophesied, and Rome the harlot of Babylon, and his reign would last as many years as the Saviour has taught days on earth." Christian clearly was influenced by his readings of Reformation histories, almost always written from the perspective of Protestants, usually Lutherans. Christian and these critics were bothered by the increasing power wielded by the papacy. Christian believed that God saw all sinners the same and that no intermediaries were needed between man and God. Pastors or church leaders were to be leaders of a flock, not men to be bowed down to or treated as religious royalty. Christian spent quite a bit of ink trying to illustrate this point, but Elise never seemed completely convinced and often gently stated that Christian should cease the discussion.[116]

The long-awaited orders finally arrived for Christian and some others of the 2nd Kansas. He recorded in his diary on April 14, 1863, "Last night we received marching orders for Fort Scott. I went out this morning and took [a] morning ramble. Everything was in its beauty and splendor and my soul was happy." Christian felt extremely glad to be away from the fort, "mostly on account of men that don't belong to our regiment and ought to be christians." Christian did make the acquaintance of an upright young man he called Britton. After much talk about religion and the Union, "we sang some hymns out of the Soldier's Hymn Book and I felt almost at home." Orrin Britton belonged to the 3rd Wisconsin Cavalry, Company A, and he was rejoining his unit at Mound City. Christian also informed Elise that he was in charge of a mess and had plenty of work to do. Most of the soldiers on the wagon train were composed of men of the 6th Kansas Cavalry.[117]

Christian was finally on the march to another military destination, and so was his brother, Henry. On April 22, Henry wrote, discussing the hardships of soldiering, including the lack of comfort of sleeping in different places almost nightly and eating scarce rations. He added, "There is only a small channel between us and the rebs. So that the pickets can speak together. We could see whole squads all day—we are right in sight of Ft. Sumpter." The Union forces could also see "the old secesh City Charleston where we expect to be ere long victorious or dead and have the last rest under its ruins.... May we meet in heaven should we not here anymore."[118]

Coincidentally, Christian wrote a letter to Elise, also dated April 22, that described his journey thus far. He had reached the vicinity of Fort Scott after passing through the towns of Olathe, Spring Hill and Paola and crossing a few small creeks and the Marais des Cygnes River. It was on the

Cavalry soldiers at Fort Scott, Kansas, circa 1863. *Courtesy Kansas State Historical Society.*

banks of the river, in 1858, that eleven free state men were marched to a ravine and shot at point-blank range by proslavery Missourians. Christian described the region as beautiful, and while stopped there, he read from his testament and drank out of the clear stream. Finally, the wagons reached Mound City, where his friend Britton departed, but not before he generously gave Christian one dollar. Christian's journey ended when the wagon train reached Fort Lincoln, a small post located twelve miles north of Fort Scott on the Little Osage River in Bourbon County. The fortification was about eighty feet long and strongly built of logs. Christian wrote that it was a large blockhouse surrounded by breastworks and "garrisoned by negro soldiers." The Osage was "a fine stream and a beautiful country on the south side of the river.... I cannot tell how long we shall remain here." Christian again expressed his thankfulness at leaving Leavenworth. "I am indeed very glad that I am away...not on account of the Post there, but more on account of the treatment we received there towards the last, by some <u>would be friends</u> and <u>Sunday christians</u>. The farther away I got from that Post the better I liked it."[119]

Captain Hugh Cameron, 2ⁿᵈ Kansas Volunteer Cavalry. Cameron lived for many years in Lawrence, Kansas, after the war. For many years, he lived as a hermit, not shaving or cutting his hair. *Courtesy Kansas State Historical Society.*

Christian wrote to his brother, elaborating on the subject of Fort Leavenworth's unsavory populace. "The easiest way to get along with such fellows and come off unharmed I find is to pass them by unnoticed and with cold indifferent contempt. If they abuse me with their filthy tongue, it is best to act as if it did not concern or mean me and if they laugh over their more vulgarity, act as if I did not hear it.... Carousing, card playing, whiskey drinking, etc., is rampant." He also remarked that men of the "basest sort" were trying to provoke him and the other good people into doing bad things. Christian confided that one reason he did not care to join his regiment stationed at Springfield, Missouri, was his personal dislike of Captain Hugh Cameron. Christian hoped to have no further contact with the captain, who was "under arrest now and his commission is likely to be broken, the Col. and nearly all the Officers, and his men are against him. 16 charges have already been preferred against him, he is one of the meanest wretches in U.S. Service.... As long as he is in Office, I shall be glad to stay away from his company."[120]

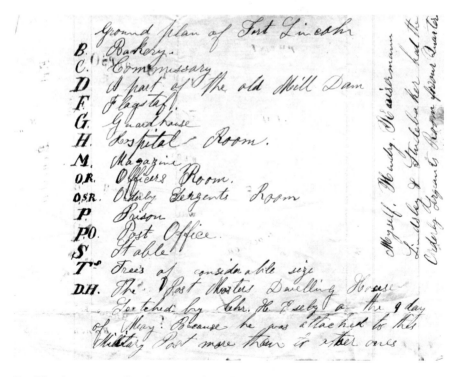

Fort Lincoln map, near Fort Scott, legend, by Christian Isely. *Courtesy Special Collections and University Archives, Wichita State University Libraries.*

Christian continued to express his views on blacks and slavery. By the spring of 1863, tens of thousands of African American soldiers had enlisted in the Union armies. These black soldiers were a source of argument among white soldiers and the American people generally. Less supportive

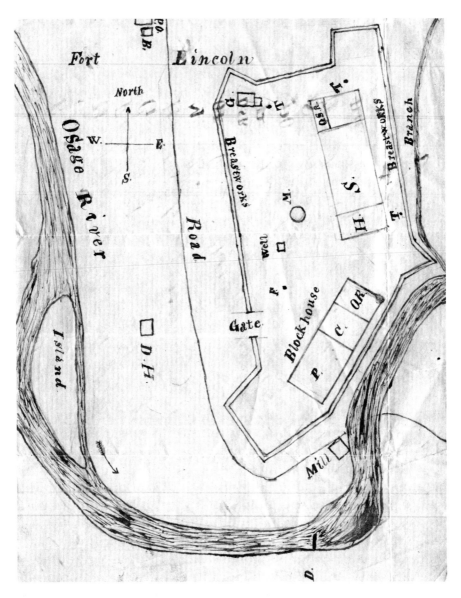

Fort Lincoln map, near Fort Scott, sketch by Christian H. Isely. *Courtesy Special Collections and University Archives, Wichita State University Libraries.*

Northerners resented Lincoln, blacks and abolitionists and blamed them for continuing senseless strife. Elise warned in her letter of June 15 that Christian should not talk as an abolitionist or discuss his support for President Lincoln. Elise expressed no disagreement with Christian's opinions but was probably less zealous in her expression of them. Instead, she realized that these remarks would trigger very negative responses from his parents and siblings. Obviously, black soldiers were even more of a contentious issue. Christian wrote a letter to Henry in May 1863, describing his encounter at Fort Lincoln with members of the 1ˢᵗ Kansas Colored Infantry, Company H, later the 79ᵗʰ United States Colored Troops. The 1ˢᵗ Kansas had been initially conceived through the efforts of Senator James Lane. By early 1863, it was a recognized unit, commanded by Lieutenant Colonel James M. Williams. His appointment was a rejection of the more radical jayhawkers Charles R. Jennison and James Montgomery. Williams led the 1ˢᵗ Kansas through much reputable service. While this unit was the fourth black regiment to enter the Union army on the basis of official muster-in dates, Kansas was the first of the free states to enroll black soldiers in service, in small units and companies, fighting in some of the first engagements of the war. In fact, the *Leavenworth Daily Conservative* reported seeing a black soldier among white soldiers in early October 1861.[121]

Christian reported as his unit arrived at the fort that they "relieved the negro soldiers next morning. Some of the boys did not like the idea very much to release the black niggers, but I went along without saying a word of discontentment." The next morning, a second lieutenant put the black soldiers "through the different evolutions and manuals of arms which they done to perfection; while the drummers and fifers played Dixie in a manner that it would do white soldiers honor. This rather beat and silenced the always over loud prejudiced faultfinders." The black soldiers soon joined their regiment at Fort Scott and were sent into active service. Christian observed that the "country in this neighborhood is very pretty and romantic and already pretty thoroughly settled but the people were made to suffer much on account of the war; it is right close to the Missouri line." Fort Lincoln was "a large square hewn black house with Stable. Wells close by and the whole is surrounded by earthen breastworks. It is stuck right in the woods and is a very lonely and solitary place but I like it very well." Christian commented that his detachment numbered only about twenty-five, and they were guarding twenty-one "secesh prisoners in custody that were left in our charge, some of them are very hard looking customers."[122]

"Strictly Loyal and Purely 'Anti Slavery'"

A letter written on May 2 by Elise evoked memories of the few years that she and Christian had spent together. "The pleasant and lovely month of May has at last come and with it many a sweet remembrance comes crowding in my mind.... I remember another May day about 3 years ago, when I pledged myself to become yours; and then there was another May day some 2 years ago when I indeed and in truth became your own Wife and you my loving Partner for life." Elise added that she felt sorry for Christian because Fort Scott did not even have a place of worship. Christian replied with his own romantic letter a few weeks later. He related a daydream about a reunion in the future. "I do hope and pray that it will come true sooner or later, and then if I don't press you warmly to my bosom and imprint burning kisses on your dear Face, then it is no use talking." In the same letter, Christian told Elise of acquiring a new horse. A fellow 2nd Kansan had picked the horse out for Christian and presented it to him. The horse was "gentle, and a splendid loper." Shortly after receiving his new mount, Christian and a mounted detachment made a fast ride from Fort Lincoln to Fort Scott. "You better believe we made the dust fly, and when we got to the Fort we looked like…Chimney sweepes, and we arrived in good season, but the wagons did not come up till late." Christian wrote that all of the men sat around the campfire, "with a slice of bacon, and a cup of tea, talking merrily over past events, and fighting with our tongues the last battles fought by Gen. Hooker in Virginia." Christian referred here to the Chancellorsville Campaign, a loss for the Union and "Fighting Joe" Hooker, but the Confederates also suffered a devastating blow when General Thomas J. "Stonewall" Jackson was accidentally mortally wounded by his own troops.[123]

On May 14, something occurred at Fort Scott that grabbed the attention of the entire garrison: a man was sentenced to be executed. The soldier belonged to the 12th Kansas, and so twelve members of the regiment were chosen by the company officers to serve as the firing squad. Their muskets were taken from them, loaded and then returned. Some of the guns had blank cartridges so that no soldier would know who fired the fatal charges. It was quite a procession as the detail moved down the street. After the convicted man was marched into an open area, "the column's right & left wing then closed in on his right & left and formed a square open only in front." Two officers approached the man and knelt while a minister prayed. His sentence was then read by a major, with the coffin in plain sight of all present. "Officers, Ministers, & Guard shook hands with him. He spoke solemnly and kindly to all." The man then fell to his knees, refused the blindfold, told his fellow soldiers that he was ready to die and "laid his hand on his left breast and told them 'to aim right there.' The order was given: Ready—aim—Fire! When no less than 6 bullets pierced and riddled his once throbbing heart. He fell motionless forward—and all was over!" Christian wrote that the man was quite repentant in death. "I wrote so much about the poor Victim [who] was lead to the place of execution like a lamb to the slaughter bench, because it so impressed me." The execution indeed had a tremendous effect on Christian, and he mentioned more than once that after witnessing it he wept silent tears. He also wrote that those present "received a lasting impression."[124]

Christian's desire to find a group of believers to join for church services intensified as the month of May wore on. He wrote on the eighteenth that the previous Sunday morning, after grazing horses, he went into town to seek out a place of worship but found none. In the evening, however, he came upon some boys of the 12th Kansas who were on their way to a religious gathering. "I went with them and much to my satisfaction, I found it quite an interesting meeting. Never did I feel more that the Spirit of God was present than I did in that humble assembly." Apparently, the congregation was made up largely of African Americans, and Christian stated that "many poor curly heads went forward with a salvation hungry soul." Christian added that there was much weeping during the service and that although they were the downtrodden ones, they "take more concern about their souls, than the boastful whites." Christian said that the service was a blessing to him and that he left it "much revived and I poured out my heart in thankfulness toward God that there is yet a black man to be found preaching the Word of God, where it is neglected by whites."[125]

Meanwhile, Elise was making her way to Christian's boyhood home in Ohio. Christian wrote in late May, "Now my Love I suppose you are no more at our own attached Home, but far away among the Ohio hills where I spent my boyhood days of dreams, hope and anticipation." Elise wrote on May 25 that she had arrived in Winesburg. "At last dearly beloved Christian your Eliza is seated in your boyhood Home to write a few lines to her own loved darling." Christian's father was different than Elise had expected, "a man of sense and good taste," and he "has a very bad cough and is extremely weak." As for her mother-in-law, Elise remarked that the "poor old woman seems to give herself a great deal of needless trouble and anxiety." Elise mentioned that she also met some other relatives, including Christian's sister and his brother Fred. "Their views are different from yours, but they are nevertheless very strong Union people…. If you or I cannot agree with them, let us always drop the subject for I wish that we could harmonize with each other." She also noted that "your people seem all to be pretty much down on the Methodists…I mean when the men folks when they speak about politics, the Methodist, the negro, and the devil seem to have a pretty close connextion." Elise closed her letter by stating that she appreciated a different likeness of Christian that he sent his mother and sister. "I had to cry when I looked at it, it looked so much like you."[126]

The Iselys separately marked their second anniversary on May 31. Christian pledged his devotion in the letter to Elise but quickly turned the subject to another execution that had occurred at Fort Scott and, again, profoundly affected him. The condemned man was a sergeant in a Missouri state militia regiment, the Union counterpart to the Confederate's Missouri state guard. He was a "tall, fine looking young fellow and if I am not mistaken was both Husband & Father. It was another very sad looking aspect." The execution was witnessed by people of all genders and races. The culprit was led to the scaffolding by two ministers, each bearing a testament in his right hand. After prayers were offered, the subject spoke to the crowd eloquently, telling all "to abide to the doctrines of the sacred Book, the Bible." A hymn was then sung by the ministers, and the condemned "shook hands with all on the scaffold, and then the rope was put about his neck by 2 soldiers and when a sign was given he was launched into eternity." The man was hanged for committing murder somewhere in Missouri, reportedly within eight miles of the fort. Shortly after the execution, Christian was among the troops ordered to Dry Wood River to reinforce Company C of the 3rd Wisconsin Cavalry. "They expected an attack that night by the Bushwhacker [Thomas] Livingston, with his band of cut throats." Livingston was creating quite a bit of havoc in the summer of 1863. Earlier in May, in southwest Missouri, he and his guerrilla band rode right into a company of the 8th Missouri State Militia cavalry, whose men mistook them for Union soldiers because the guerrillas were wearing Union uniforms. This tactic was fairly common, and it infuriated Union commanders to the extent that when caught, most guerrillas were shot on the spot. Christian finished his letter by stating that while they had been on a good tramp, no bushwhackers were found.[127]

Elise wrote a letter of her own on their anniversary. "You have no idea my Christian, how dear you are to me, and how often I think of you and look at your likeness with the fondest affection." She next discussed some difficulties that she experienced. "I have already mentioned to you in some of my former letters that I was not quite well…. I took very sick all at once with a kind of labouring pains…. I look very poor and pale and I am also weak after such a loss of blood." Happily, she was feeling much better, and she was again able to do some work. Elise commented, "I have not yet been homesick and only a little lonesome after you my own Christian." Due no doubt to her surroundings, Elise expressed her thoughts on religious toleration. "Dearest Love, I have been thinking of late, how thankful we ought to be to our Heavenly Father that he has opened our eyes and given us hearts wide enough to love all our different denominational brethren in Christ and that we are not so full of prejudices against others that do not think as we do."

Obviously, much of the talk around the Isely home focused on religion, and according to Elise, most of it was negative in tone. Later in the same letter, she stated, "A great deal is said here about Politics and Religion but the Lord has blessed me with a peaceful heart and tongue." Still, she reported, Christian's parents were quite concerned about their boys in uniform. "Your Father makes a special prayer for his 2 sons in the army every night." Elise ended on a note of instruction. "When you write, always write separate what you wish me to keep for myself, so that I can give my letters to read to your people." A letter written a week later contained an even more revealing statement about Christian's family. Elise divulged that "they are nevertheless a curious kind of people.... I think if the love has grown cold by any, it is here for very little love is manifested for others and their charity has room in a small place." Elise clearly felt a need to share these intimate observations with her husband.[128]

Christian penned a letter on June 8 from camp near Fort Scott. The previous eight days had been exciting ones. After over a year and a half in the army, Christian finally came face to face with the enemy. He had been on two tramps. The first to the northeast, down the valley of the Marmaton River and about forty miles into Missouri. The second trek was to the southwest, into Osage country. Christian stated that he could not be as descriptive as he would like, for then his letter would be too long. He revealed that "I have come in contact with what might have extinguished the vitals of your won Christian, and I cannot see any other cause that covered my defenceless head in the moment of danger, but the merciful hand that has ever been nigh to protect and to keep me from childhood up to the present day, even the hand of my merciful God. And thus I am still in the Land of mortal man to tell my own story to my own Darling Love." The tale began on June 2, when an order was given that every man should feed his horse a double ration of corn. After the sun went down, forty men saddled up and headed toward the east end of town, where they united with Captain Moore and six men of the 3rd Wisconsin Cavalry. "The Capt. told us to march quietly along and neither speak loud nor make any noise."

Christian said that the men moved "all as still as death" until they had traveled about six miles from town, where they were reinforced by thirty-five troopers of the 6th Kansas Cavalry. After traveling most of the night, Christian reported that "we divided out in 3 parts, our Lieut. went with us. Then all at once the command was given to gallop, when we all darted off like fury, and on the top of a hill we all met coming in from every direction and surrounded a log house, where we expected to catch some bushwhackers, but found only 3 women." After a short rest in the woods, the men resumed their ride. "We ran right on some of those demons & ragged wretches and you better believe they hunted their holes mighty quick. And we pursued them as fast as we could." Christian got somewhat separated from the rest of his men and found one of the enemy concealed in the bush. Just as Christian caught up to him, the bushwhacker turned around "with a big double barreled shot gun in his hands, and I was neither ready nor prepared to fire my gun or rifle as quick as he could have done, and without thinking long what I should do, I just put the spurs to my horse and went out through the timber & brush." Christian wrote that he "expected a shot every minute but happily received none." After rejoining his unit, Christian told the story, and immediately the balance of his men gave chase in the direction of the bushwhacker. "I was again the first one that seen him but he was already more than 50 yards from his former place." Christian pointed toward him, and Lieutenant Cosgrove shot at him "and made him sing out enough." The captain then questioned the bushwhacker, who answered very defiantly. "He was then put on a horse that we captured from them and some of [the] boys took him a little to one side. The Capt. told them to take care of him and they of course understood what it meant and sent a little lead through his infernal head." Christian wrote that he did not know if any other bushwhackers were killed in the raid, and all of his detachment returned to the fort safely.[129]

A little less than a week later, Christian told of his episode regarding the Osage Indians. Christian left Fort Scott with forty men, including twenty-five Indians. According to Christian, three of the Indians were Shawnees, and two of them knew some English. After quite a trip, the detachment arrived at the Osage Mission on June 5. The mission was run by Catholics, and Christian expressed his sadness that the Indians were being "educated in superstition." Regardless, the purpose of the expedition was to "do the Indians honor for noted bravery in defence of our dear Union's cause and also to distribute presents among them as rewards for merit, in pursuing a band of guerilla bushwhackers over 3 miles that ventured into their Lands." The Indians killed many rebels and lost two of their own "valiant braves."

The Osages met "us on the Prairie, in their own wild way, and surrounded us. They came upon us from every direction & as if they came out of the ground flying over the Prairie like an arrow through the air." The soldiers were put in a line, and the Indians rode around them like a "raging whirlpool, caused by angry waves, yelling their old wild warwhoops, and as they were then going it, we discharged our rifles in the air as a salute, which pleased them not a little." Christian ended his letter by talking of the beauty of the Neosho Valley, the streams and flowers. "I wish you could have been there with me…. That was indeed a very interesting and romantic thing for me."[130]

Slavery, Methodists, Catholics, Copperheads and whether or not the pope was the Antichrist were recurring themes in the Isely letters, especially through the summer of 1863. One of the Copperheads' shortcomings, according to Christian, was that they "never read a thoroughly loyal paper. They never read anything else but such that suits their own taste." They chose papers that were full of prejudice, intolerance and tainted information. Christian entreated Elise not to argue openly with them but never to agree with them either; instead, her sentiments must remain "strictly Loyal and purely "Anti Slavery." Christian stated that the more he witnessed the bitter fruits of secession and slavery, "the more I am convinced, that it is an outrage that was born in no other place outside of hell & with hellish demons. Strict Loyalty & Anti Slavery principles and a profound repentance before God can safe[guard] our country and it will do it too, no matter how strong the opposition now may appear to be."[131]

Elise wrote a revealing letter to Christian on June 15 that addressed some of the divisive feelings and sentiments among the people in Ohio. By the summer of 1863, Elise was emerging as the referee between Christian's strong antislavery, pro-Union stances and the ambivalence or Copperheadism of his various family members. Elise had recently accompanied Christian's mother to visit his sister Barbara; brother Fred; and sister-in-law, Pauline. Elise stated that while she wished Christian were out of the army, he would not be happy in Ohio because one could "not look with composure at the divisions and hatred which fiends place among the different denominations of Union people." Elise warned Christian that if he wrote to Fred again, "don't say anything about Pre[sident] Lincoln. They all dislike him very much here and if you should say anything about the negroes, express yourself in a manner to show that you are not an Abolitionist." Elise gently added, "I don't wish to dictate… what you should do or write…but it is my ardent wish that you should be on good terms with your relatives, especially because I am here. I would like to not hear anything against you." Near the end of the letter, Elise described how she was able to tolerate the separation and anxiety that she experienced. "Therefore, let us constantly pray for each other that we may become more like unto the meek and lowly Jesus and then we will not fail to be as we ought to all men. I have lived nearer to God of late than ever." When alone, "Sweet passages of Scripture always come to my mind and I sometimes…work with my hands and my soul seems to almost have left this vale of tears."[132]

On June 15, Christian set off on another foray. Along with forty members of the 3rd Wisconsin Cavalry, Company C, orders were issued to head in a southeasterly direction "on a regular bushwhacker scout." Christian reported that the entire detachment consisted of seventy men. "We arrived at the timber west of Lamar, but did not cross over to town, that we might not be seen by any body, in order to easier slap on the [Bushwackers]." The following morning, Wednesday, June 17, Christian was sent out with eleven men and a guide, but they found nothing except a large orchard, full of cherry trees, of which he wrote that we "at[e] to our heart's content." A day later, the march continued, and again finding no rebels, Christian wrote that they commenced gathering up their stock: "their horses, oxen, milk cows & calves." It was a beautiful country, and by Thursday evening, the detachment was about fifteen miles east of Carthage, Missouri.

On that evening, as the men camped and Christian engaged in guard detail, a squad of 2nd Kansas men was sent out to scout and report back. The men advanced no more than a quarter mile from camp when "they were fired upon from the bush." Two of the troopers were thrown from their horses. "One of them, however got into camp, but the other one we could not find neither dead or alive. He was a very nice boy and we are very sorry for him. His name was Peter Basey." The entire command saddled up, expecting an attack at any moment. They "got inside of the ruins of the brick court house that was burned down by the rebels because they were whip there once before. No remonstrance however was made during the night and yesterday morning, we started for Ft. Scott." The men arrived safely back at Fort Scott. Peter Basey, it turned out, "was taken prisoner and paroled." Christian wrote that he was the first one to approach Basey when he came back, and Basey had a "God Bless You" on his lips. "He looked quite poor and care worn."[133]

As the Civil War dragged on, and personal tragedies and difficulties besieged the Iselys, Christian lost none of his dedication to the Union cause. In fact, his conviction seemingly grew with the more adversity he faced. Still, he fought loneliness along with the enemy. He always viewed the Iselys' travails as a test of their faith in God. If they and others like them kept the faith and served the cause, the Union would be preserved. As he wrote in the summer of 1863, "I have not now, nor never had the remotest doubt, that not all things will finally come right and in favor of this people and Government, although we can not now see it, in that light. It is our duty to hope and wait patiently till that happy day comes about, and…give our bleeding Land & Country our heartiest support and assistance."[134]

CHAPTER 8

"I PREPARED MYSELF FOR THE WORST"

During the summer of 1863, as Christian underwent a taste of battle, Elise was in Ohio, withstanding an onslaught of political rhetoric that ran counter to her beliefs. "Peace Democrats" (Copperheads) were bewildering to Elise. Some of the Ohio people she came into contact with were totally indifferent to the outcome of the war. "Unlike the Kansans and Missourians, who were intensely partisan on one side or the other, Ohio had thousands with no strong desire to preserve the Union or to do away with slavery." Elise wrote that many were opposed to the idea of coercing the South, and this led to much opposition to the military draft. Christian's parents often asked Elise to read his letters aloud. In doing so, she generally had to omit certain portions, which made Elise feel as though she was lying to the elder Iselys. In the letter detailing the killing of the bushwhacker, for instance, Elise stated only that they took care of him. She wrote to Christian that "your Father thinks it is a dreadful thing to kill rebels. But I don't think any about here would think very hard of it if the so called Abolitionists were all killed." Elise explained that Christian should have no fear that she would turn into a Copperhead. "If I could see that these people are better than others, it would be an inducement, but I have no reason in the least to take their side."[135]

What made Elise's task much more difficult was that she could not speak openly. In late June, she wrote that she had gone into the town of Winesburg, where she finally came upon a truly loyal person. The event occurred in the post office, and the woman she spoke with was the postmaster's wife. Fearful of answering certain questions, Elise began by being very guarded in her conversation. The woman inquired how things were going with the war in the West, and Elise responded that it was better there since the people were either wholly loyal or wholly rebel and "that there were not so many half-rebels." A frank exchange ensued, and Elise wrote that if "she is not hard on rebels, then nobody is." Interestingly enough, Elise heard from Christian's parents that they did not care for the new postmaster because he was an abolitionist. Elise said nothing to them about her new friend. According to Elise, "all truly loyal people are called Blacks and Abolitionists, I am one too, but of course my tongue is silent and will have to be, if utter necessity does not compel me to speak." If anyone knew what she was writing, "they would hate [me] instead of loving me…. I sometimes begin to doubt if people possessed with so little love for others can be Christians, but there is no use arguing or speaking a word against it for it would just be throwing oil into the fire." Elise wrote that having to keep her feelings inside, among such distrustful people, was difficult. "I have to swallow it all and keep it all for myself and therefore, you have no idea how much good it does me to tell you a little." As difficult as the circumstances were, Elise ascribed them all to God's plan for her life. She was convinced that her mission in Ohio was one of love and peace. "Please love, pray for me that I may be as wise and prudent as a serpent and as simple as a dove for now."[136]

Christian, by early July, perceived that Elise was in a difficult position, trying to maintain peace within the family by withholding her true feelings. Christian wrote that the entire situation sickened him, and he hoped that Elise's heart and soul would not be crushed by their "uncharitable prejudice." One particular letter that Christian received from his brother was especially disturbing. Christian wrote that if Fred called this a Union letter, "as he pleases to term it…I am sadly grieved that he has become so deluded." Everything that they write, claimed Christian, was against the Union government and evinced no love for their country. "They are nothing else but the devoted servants of Jeff. Davis & his conspiracy, if not alltogether the Devil's own Agents." Apparently, Fred asked Christian to answer some questions about the war. Christian wrote to Elise, however, that he would refrain from answering because to do so would result in a "stern remonstrance." He also stated that "I do not wish to discuss politics with them for they could not bear my expressions, and experience would not permit me to not ascent [sic] to any of their absurdities. But they can not cease throwing out their detestable insinuations, and so I will quit writing to them." Christian noted that he could find others to write to who will "consider themselves quite honored when they get a letter…and they also appreciate my views very much."[137]

Christian's long letter, written over a period of two days, addressed Elise's previously expressed concerns. "You also state that I should not write this thing nor mention that thing, nor speak in favor of Lincoln, etc. Now if I write at all, I will do it concienciously, strictly adhering to truth & integrity." Christian refused to be muted in his expressions of loyalty to the Northern cause. His guideposts were the "blessed teachings of our meek & lowly Redeemer, Jesus, our Lord & Master." Remaining quiet, argued Christian, was not effective, as "radical measures" were needed. Christian maintained that while the Union government might not be perfect, it was their duty to support it as true "Loyal Patriots." Christian explained why loyalty to the cause was especially important. "They surely cannot be both right or both wrong and I take it for granted that our Government & Abraham Lincoln is right and the rebel conspiracy & Jeff Davis wrong. I give my hearty support to the former." Christian wrote, "I have no right to abuse our Government and those that govern it because they have faults, nor have I a right to desert it in this time of distress. No man has a right to forsake his Wife…because she has become helplessly sick." Those opposed to the government were "poor, short-sighted people." If they argued that President Lincoln was overstepping his constitutional authority through wartime legislation, Christian disagreed, stating that "as the evil progresses, so it assumes a new and different aspect and new Laws have to be made to meet and check the malady."[138]

Christian encouraged Elise to stay loyal and do everything in her power for the Union cause. "Hence I claim that Abe Lincoln needs and deserves all the support that possibly can be rendered him by all the truly Loyal & Patriotic hearts, and it is also your Duty to take a firm stand in his and our country's behalf." Christian noted that Elise had never been afraid to speak her mind previously. "Are you growing faint now? And if it should get to hot for you in this hotbed of copperheads, then just let me know and I will try to send you enough money to bring you back to Missouri." Christian stated that Americans were divided into five classes. The first "embraces all the good people, all true Christian[s], and all true Patriots" supporting the Union. These individuals were loyal, undivided in their love and support, and they pray, weep and fight for the cause. The second class came out boldly for the Confederacy and fought manfully against the Union "in a fair warfare & fair manner." The third class were those who continually found fault with the Union government "yet are to[o] cowardly to join the secesh army." The fourth class were "all those that pretend to fight in a sneaking manner like the Bushwhackers against any soldiers." The fifth class "sneak about at home and try to injure our cause all they can while they try to make all the money they can off of the Government…. Now to which class all should belong is more than self evident." Of course, Christian placed most of his Ohio relatives in either the third or fifth classes. "They pour oil into the fire" by abusing the government and discouraging enlistment. "The southerners do not want any thing better than the continual contention in the north." Discouraging letters written by antiwar Northerners had a terrible effect on soldiers. Christian wrote that if they truly cared, they could at least hold their tongues. Conversely, Christian encouraged Elise on behalf of our "bleeding Land & Country" to "write cheerful encouraging letters to the soldiers."[139]

The summer was an active one for Christian, who remained stationed at Fort Scott. In early July, he wrote that on a six-day tramp into Missouri, the Union soldiers ran into some bushwhackers at an area near Clear and Horse Creeks; at least one bushwhacker was killed, while none of his detachment was injured. "They tried very hard to kill some of our number," but all returned "safe & well into camp again with about 500 heads of horses, cattle & sheep, confiscated property." Christian participated in a number of similar expeditions, all of which made a strong impression on him. Some of these forays were made with small detachments, which increased the possibility of vicious attacks by irregulars. On July 7, Christian left Fort Scott for Springfield, Missouri, where he rejoined his regiment for the first time since early in the war. As Christian arrived, a twin celebration over the fall of Vicksburg and the victory at Gettysburg had just ended. Christian wrote that the trip to Springfield was full of scenic countryside, especially as they approached the western edge of the Ozark Mountains, but much of what they saw was in ruin. "Springfield lies on a very beautiful valley, mostly prairie land, but there is timber seen in all directions. It is a quite fine looking town yet, but it has many marks of war." One of the first to greet Christian was Colonel William F. Cloud of the 2nd Kansas. "Never a man received more affectionately and friendly than he did. He said, 'I am so glad to see you and see that you look so well,' and after the salutations were exchanged, he smilingly ask[ed], 'How is Mrs. Isely and where is she.'" Cloud told Christian that his family had also visited Ohio the past winter but were now in Springfield. Christian wrote that Cloud was the same "keen looking long haired man yet as when you seen him."[140]

Elise responded to Christian on July 16, warning him that use of the word "Copperhead" stirred up emotions in the household. The mere mention of it caused his father much pain. Moreover, she warned Christian not to write that he and Henry agreed on wartime issues because it exposed both brothers to the family's criticism. She also added that she pitied Henry, since he rarely received a cheerful letter from home. "They are so intoxicated with treason and rebelion, and in such a manner that they are not aware of the least speck of their hateful malady." Elise was certain, though, that Christian's mother truly cared about him. "Her poor old heart beats warmly for you of which I have been convinced more than once." In early August, Elise informed Christian that Henry had been in some intense combat at Charleston. Elise reported that "half of his Co[mpany] were killed and wounded, but thanks be to God he was not hurt, but it makes me feel sad to state that they did not gain much." Elise was unaware of the details, but Henry had participated in a most terrible campaign. His unit was part of the assault on Fort Wagner, where thousands were lost, including large numbers of the 54th Massachusetts, an African American regiment. Elise concluded her letter by telling Christian how much he meant to her. "Never Beloved, have you been dearer to me than of late and never have I been more willing to give you in the behalf of our dear Bleeding land in its present struggle." Elise regretted that she could do no more than write cheering letters to solders. "When I think of the poor neglected wounded and suffering in the hospitals throughout the land, it makes me feel very sad indeed that I can do nothing for some of them." Something she did do almost unceasingly was "shed sympathizing tears in their behalf and I pray for them. I think if some of our noble boys knew how high they stand in their esteem it would often be the means of encouraging them in their sore trials and hardships."[141]

As Elise was writing her letter full of patriotic fervor, she had no idea that Christian had recently engaged the enemy. He wrote that same day, August 2, from camp near Cassville, Missouri, "It pleased God to spare & protect me thus far and I have again the happy priviledge to Address you, and call you mine." Before Christian related the details of the march, he informed Elise that, repeatedly, when alone or on picket or guard duty, his thoughts were completely of her. When last they saw each other, she "gave me to understand by her actions, words, & looks, that I possessed no small portion of her loving heart...how happy would we be, if the coming New Year had a happy meeting in store for us?" Christian then turned his attention to the war. "Last Friday morning ten of us 2nd Kan. Boys in command of a Sergt. were ordered to mount our horses and report to Head Quarters." Upon arriving there, the men were told that they were to escort about a dozen Confederates under a flag of truce to Fayetteville, Arkansas, about sixty miles distant. The Union detachment, under Lieutenant Bard of the 1st Arkansas, was to link up with about two hundred men of the 1st Arkansas and the 2nd Kansas. However, when they arrived within about fifteen miles of Fayetteville, they were told by some locals that four hundred rebels, camped in the area, had driven off the Union force. Interestingly enough, stuck in this precarious position, the rebels being escorted kindly told the Union men that they would lead them back to safety. Christian wrote that "we chatted, drank coffee, and stood Guard together and acted like the best kind of Friends together." However, some of the men who were going to escort them to safety apparently tipped off other Confederates in the area. In an area near the Pea Ridge battlefield, behind some cliffs and bushes on a high rock, "a gang lay in wait for us, we could not see anybody, but as we passed along they fired on us a murderous volley, but as a merciful God would have it, no one got hurt."

Next to Christian during this ordeal was a good friend named John W. Hendry, also of Company F. Hendry's horse was shot but rose again, and Hendry remounted, "and as we could not do any good by returning the fire, we tried to get out of the wilderness as fast as our horses could carry us, for we did not know how soon we would be fired on again." The "hollow," or enclosed area in which the battle began, was six miles in length. Christian wrote that they took off with speed, but before he could escape, his horse gave out. "But the Lieut. God bless him, he is a very kind man. Him and the Boys helped me along the best they could when I had to leave my poor horse." The men returned safely into camp, and Christian wrote that "I have thanked God for his kind protection."[142]

Another expedition of 2nd Kansas men was not as lucky. Christian wrote on August 3 that another group on a scout toward Fayetteville had met a bad fate. Three men—John Ingalls, John Clayton and James Tidwell—had been shot. Clayton was killed. Ingalls received a bullet through the neck but appeared to be recovering, and Tidwell, who was a close friend, was shot five times and "may die yet. I shall be very sorry for him. All this was done by Bushwhackers, and yet those wretches have the sympathy of copperheads!!!" Christian wrote in his diary a few days later, "I was sitting up with Jim Tidwell last night. This morning, I had a fine season of prayer…. I am glad poor Jim is getting better." Christian also spent an evening comforting the injured Ingalls, who likewise survived his wounds. Christian wrote that Ingalls "is a very bad fellow and cause me much grief at Ft. Scott & Lincoln, but I forgave him all and had a chance to return good for evil. He is quite kind to me now." While visiting Tidwell and Ingalls, Christian wrote that he could not help think of Henry, "probably suffering in the same manner and again I thought how thankful he would be if some kind heart and hand was watching over him." The newspaper account of the attack on Fort Wagner made Christian "almost sick when I first read it." As he realized his brother might be "among the slain or wounded, I could hardly bear the thought for a long time. But I retired into the woods for secret prayer, and afterwards felt much relieved, and it seemed to me almost certain that our dear Brother is still alive and I cannot now believe otherwise."[143]

Christian, in his letters of early August, again returned to his family's political disputes and how they affected Elise and the Northern fighting men. He encouraged Elise not to grow fainthearted or silent. In regard to Elise's writing that his mother would prefer to hear nothing from them about politics, Christian wrote, "Now I hope you have not promised her any such thing, for if you have, you violated your promise, and that you know would be wrong." He added that Elise should tell his family that she possessed a "love of freedom of press, freedom of speech, & freedom of thought. But not for the purpose of injuring any body, nor the purpose of thwarting nor slandering the Government and its gallant upholders, like the copperheads" did. Christian encouraged Elise to stand her ground and not be afraid. Those against the government will fall to destruction, as "blind leaders of the blind" will "fall in the ditch." He stated that he was very sorry that Elise had to "endure so much from the unworthy, cowardly, sneaking copperheads; it makes my blood boil when I hear of their treachery." The situation had deteriorated to the point that Elise encouraged Christian not to come to Ohio should he be mustered out early. "I had no idea of their thoughts toward truly loyal persons and pen and ink cannot express their views and as you say writing is too limited." Elise continued, "They curse all the upholders of the Gov., they abuse everything that at least seems to me to be right and I don't think there are any much worse than your own relatives." Still, Elise urged Christian to be "patient and forbear with them" because they were his parents.[144]

On August 3, Christian wrote of an unpleasant episode in his military life. For more than a year, he had served as a corporal, but in the summer of 1863, he was reduced in rank. It was not a subject that Christian discussed in great detail, but he attributed the demotion to Captain Hugh Cameron. Cameron had been detached from the regiment for quite some time and had come up on many charges, and apparently Christian was one of the men who gave a statement regarding Cameron's abuses. Christian wrote that "it makes no difference to me." If Cameron returned to the regiment,

Christian would not serve under him as a noncommissioned officer. "He thought probably that he done me a great injury, but I don't happen to look at it in that light."[145]

Henry Isely wrote to Christian from the regimental hospital on Morris Island, South Carolina, on September 2, 1863. Henry took the opportunity to answer some of the claims of "copperheadism" in addition to providing a recapitulation of the past summer's struggles. Apparently, Christian had referred to Winesburg, Ohio, as a "Copperhead hole." Henry took Christian to task, reminding him that Winesburg had sent many of its sons into the army, including two who "were killed in the recent charge before the walls of Ft. Wagner.... They are with few exceptions, so unlucky all to have been democrats." Henry made the argument that such Democrats served the Union well, even "risking their life for the sake of their country, yet they have the honor of being called Copperhead." Henry had received a letter from their mutual friend John Kunzli, who claimed to be the only loyal man remaining in Holmes County, Ohio. Henry argued that a loyal person does not run down someone else's character. "I bore it patiently, yet it gave me many a sad hour, and often had to hear many an unpleasant word. May God forgive him!"

Henry then turned his attention to the events of July 18, when the 67th Ohio made its deadly charge on Fort Wagner. "The field was strewn over with hundreds of dead and wounded and as we passed along, the moans rising of the dieing and cries of the wounded could be heard through the terrible sounding of artillery." Still, amid all of the horror, Henry reported that "the flag of our reg. was planted on the fort although the bearer had fallen and all the color guards had been wounded except one or two. This besides the 6th Conn. of the 1st Brigade were the only ones brought on the fort." Henry related that his colonel, lieutenant colonel, adjutant and almost all of the line officers were killed or wounded. Company C, in fact, "took 29 men including officers in the battle and brought 14 out safe, to the latter through the grace and protection of Providence I can count myself." Henry added that "many fell to my right and left, but I came out unharmed, the honor to God alone." Since the failed assault on Fort Wagner, Henry had contracted typhoid fever. As September began, he was just beginning to regain his health.[146]

The letter Henry wrote on September 2 was not received by Christian for a few weeks. By that time, Christian, too, had "seen the elephant." He fully experienced the face of battle, a moment every soldier anticipates and dreads. His hastily written letter, dated September 5, told the tale that "we left Camp McNeil on Friday the 14th early, and arrived at Bentonville, Ark. that evening. From there, we went to Fayetteville, and then over the Prairie Grove battle ground to Rays [Rhea's] Mill." Once at Rhea's Mill, it was reported that General James Blunt was being "driven out of Ft. Gibson," and the 2nd Kansas "made straight for the latter place; but when we got there the rebels under Gen. Cooper had retreated." After a few days, it was decided to mount a pursuit of the enemy. The chase led to Perryville in the Choctaw nation, a "days march south of [the] Canadian" river, almost down to Texas. "They made a stand at Perryville and fired into our advance with their Artillery, but they were soon driven out shot & shell sent after them; but it became dark and we could not pursue them any more that night." After camping the night, the commanders decided to discontinue the pursuit. "Our troops were very tired and the horses used up, the roads very dusty, the weather extremely hot, and water poor and scarce, and so we destroyed the town and rebel property, and turned back next morning, took up our march for Ft. Smith." When the men neared the fort, Colonel Cloud, based on new intelligence, decided to chase after the rebels again. The pursuing force consisted of the "2nd Kas., 6th Mo. & Rabs Battery, we gave a warm pursued and run on their rear at about 2 o'clock and soon got into a hot engagement with them, but thanks to God, we came out best. We lost 15 wounded & killed." Christian ended his letter by sadly reporting that his good friend, Corporal William Staatz, was killed in the action. The march took quite a physical toll—the men were in the saddle for nearly three weeks, surviving on about one-fourth rations the entire time.[147]

The military action that Christian described in his letter was known as the Battle of Backbone Mountain or the Devil's Backbone. William Staatz was apparently a close friend of Christian's because his name is mentioned on a few occasions. In a letter dated August 30, 1863, Elise remarked to Christian that when "you write about your friends H. and Statz please put it separately." The reason for the request of a separate sheet is not apparent, but it's possible that they shared Christian's political views and so therefore he quoted them from time to time. This, of course, would have angered his parents. Staatz was not the battle's only casualty. Official records of the adjutant general of Kansas list two killed and four wounded. The other fatality was Captain Edward Lines, of Company C, whose unit was ambushed. Of the four wounded men, Frank Falkner, also of Company C, died on September 7 as a result of his wounds.[148]

A few days later, Christian gave a detailed account of what occurred at the Devil's Backbone. The 2nd Kansas was in the advance of that day. "The scouts and Col. Cloud's body guard, Company C, were in the extreme front, then it was our Co., and I was 3rd in number [at the advance] of our Co., I prepared myself for the worst." The Confederates were fast retreating toward the Sugar Loaf Mountains, and Colonel Cloud decided to give chase. Christian informed Elise that the Union forces numbered between 800 and 1,000, while the rebels were reportedly 2,400 strong. As they pursued the rebels, many stragglers from the Confederate ranks were captured. Shortly after pausing to water horses, a tremendous "fire of musketry opened on Co. 'C.' A regiment of rebs placed themselves on one side of the road in a cornfield and another in the woods & brushes, on the other side and it is very strange that one man of Co. 'C' escaped." Christian reported that Staatz was killed instantly, and "the Captain and one private mortally wounded. 2 of our Co. were wounded besides 2 others of other companies were mortally wounded."

The whole of the regiment next fell into line and "advanced and dismounted and formed into line of battle and drove the rebels about a mile." Seven companies of the regiment were engaged, in all about 300 men. Company C, he stated, was entirely "hors du [de] combat," or militarily disabled. Much of the rest of the battle was "chiefly done with artillery…. Their artillery fired did not do us much damage." Christian maintained in his letter that had they possessed more ammunition, "or we ourselves had not been exhausted, we could have distroyed that whole rebel force." Major Samuel J. Crawford, later a general and wartime Kansas governor, wrote that the Confederate forces commenced the battle by concealing themselves in the bushes with the "purpose of assassination." Crawford noted that much of the warfare in the West began with an ambush. Surely, this instilled a feeling of anxiety and retribution among soldiers who were on the receiving end of such attacks. Crawford added, "This was a species of warfare to which the Second Kansas never condescended. That regiment fought in the open and was always there at the beginning and the ending, but never once did any soldier of the regiment sneak around in the brush and shoot an enemy in the back."[149]

The Battle of Backbone Mountain, Christian's true baptism of fire, was certainly not significant by Civil War standards. It occurred in Sebastian County, Arkansas, and followed the Battle of Honey Springs, in Indian Territory. General James Blunt, at Fort Smith, ordered Colonel William F. Cloud to pursue retreating Confederates. Cloud, with about 1,500 men composing the 2nd Kansas, 6th Missouri Cavalry and two sections of Rabb's 2nd Indiana Battery, clashed with 1,200 Arkansas soldiers commanded by Confederate general William Cabell. The engagement lasted about three hours before the Confederates resumed their retreat and headed in disorder for Waldron, Arkansas. Devil's Backbone was a ridge in the Ouachita Mountains, sixteen miles south of Fort Smith. Total casualties ranged from 31 to 81. All accounts put Union casualties between 14 and 16, demonstrating Christian's estimate of 15 to be quite correct. Confederate casualties are much more difficult to calculate. Some sources list them at 17, while others believe the number to be closer to 65. The discrepancy can partly be explained by the number of Confederate deserters who surrendered in the days that followed the battle and pursuit.[150]

Elise wrote affectionately on September 6, "Pen and ink cannot express how fondly you are cherished by me, my poor Christian." After expressing her hope that "the time will come when war shall be heard no more," she turned to a notorious episode of the border war. She shared with Christian a newspaper report of the terrible massacre at Lawrence, Kansas, on August 21, 1863. William C. Quantrill, a name that many Kansas soldiers and border residents had already learned to fear, led an early morning raid of 450 Confederate Partisan Rangers on Lawrence, a symbol of abolitionist and antislavery sentiment. In roughly three hours, Quantrill and his men shot and murdered at least 150 men and boys before riding off at the approach of Federal soldiers. Quantrill claimed that the raid was in retribution for crimes committed by Kansas, including its treatment of civilians linked to Quantrill's guerrillas. Most viewed the brutal assault on civilians as evil and beneath the conduct of any civilized society, even in wartime. Somewhat surprisingly, Christian and Elise make relatively little mention of the massacre, remarking simply that it was horrendous and unforgivable.[151]

The Lawrence raid and Union victories were beginning to push fence sitters in Kansas and Missouri to side with the Union. Worst of all for Quantrill and the region's Southern sympathizers, the massacre prompted Union brigadier general Thomas Ewing, later a major general in the Department of Kansas, to issue General Order No. 11, which forced civilians to evacuate four specific border counties in Missouri that provided safe haven for bushwhackers and guerrillas. The order stated that people residing in Jackson, Cass, Bates and Vernon Counties, with the exception of those living within one mile of Independence, Hickman Mills, Pleasant Hill, Harrisonville or Kansas City, were to leave their homes by September 9, 1863. If residents of the region were deemed to be loyal by the military authorities, they could remain in their homes. The evacuation was both a response to the massacre and an attempt to deprive the bushwhackers of their support areas. Order No. 11 was likely issued for various reasons.

It was meant to prevent further raids and calm the people of Kansas. Many Kansans were calling for an immediate response. If the military or government did not act, citizens or mobs might take justice into their own hands, causing even more chaos. Revenge and response were on the minds of many Kansans in the wake of the massacre. Many wondered how the military authorities could have allowed such an atrocity to have occurred. Aggressive action was called for not only by the public but also by Senator James Lane. Lane undoubtedly pressured Ewing into quickly implementing an aggressive policy. Certainly, another motive was General Ewing's own ambition, personal and political.[152]

For weeks following the Battle of Backbone Mountain, rebel refugees made their way to Union lines. Christian made multiple references to the "Mountain Feds" who also came into the Union camp. These loyal Union men had kept themselves concealed in the mountains when Confederates controlled the region. "I wish the copperheads of Ohio could hear these Deserters & Refugees talk awhile. If it would not touch their hearts to sympathy and eyes to tears, and inspire them with true patriotism." Exposure to these suffering, yet loyal, mountain people would cure the Copperheads' "sore malady"—or they "ought to be candidates for the insane asylum." For years, armies had foraged the livestock, poultry and grain of these loyal mountain people. Guerrilla bands had plundered their households, violated their women and "carried off their valuables." By the spring of 1864, more than 1,500 of these dispossessed Unionists and 300 slaves had gathered at Fort Smith. Many of the loyal refugees were more than willing to take up arms for the Union cause. Colonel Cloud wrote that several hundred pleaded with him "to stand by them and keep them from being taken by the [Confederate] conscript officers or from being taken into the Rebel Army," because many of them had "recently deserted."[153]

Christian wrote that some of the erstwhile rebels who gave themselves up in late 1863 had never wanted to serve in the Confederacy. "Most of them have been conscripted into the rebel service and are, and always have been heart & soul, Union men. They often come by whole companies." These soldiers, who never cared that much for the Southern cause, "are so glad to come back under the dear old flag." Cloud wrote that on his journey to Dardanelle, Arkansas, in late September, three hundred soldiers in Confederate uniforms came in with "Stars and Stripes flying, and cheers for the Union." They had fought against Cloud at Backbone Mountain but now were willing to fight for the Union. These former Confederate soldiers may have been, as Christian believed, wholly pro-Union from the outset of the war, but some also were hungry, weary and tired of being pursued. Christian was impressed with the way Colonel Cloud handled himself, often referring to his honesty and fairness. A week after the fight at Backbone Mountain, Christian wrote, "That Cloud is a dashing little fellow."[154]

At the end of September, Elise informed Christian that it made her feel sad that Staatz "had to lose his life and that you lost so good a friend. It makes me shed tears while I write this, but he has gone Home and we will meet him there, won't we Love?" Elise then told Christian that if no one else had written Staatz's family, he should "state the particulars of his death, and tell them what a good freind he has been to you." Should tragedy ever befall Christian, Elise asserted, "I would feel very grateful to the one that would have the kindness to write it to me, but I trust and pray to God that such may not be my lot. Really, I don't know how I could survive your loss." Elise characteristically committed Christian's fate to God and closed with a benediction.[155]

A week later, Elise again entreated Christian to refrain from mentioning politics in his letters to Ohio. At the same time, she vented her own frustrations and anxieties regarding the "loyal" and "disloyal" inhabitants of Holmes County. All who speak out in favor of the Northern cause were slandered by the Copperheads. One particular woman, an older Swiss lady, "is a good Christian and also a patriot, but shamefully abused, despised, and slandered by the vile Copperheads." Elise claimed that if Christian could hear his parents and brother Fred talk, "it would make your very blood boil for it comes very near making mine boil. It at least makes my heart ache with pain to hear the shameful slander with which they insult our cause and country. I could stand it no longer and therefore came up stairs." Most painfully, they "quote the scripture and think they are the only good. We are fanatics, folks, blind, Black, Abolitionist. If you saw the papers they read, you wouldn't be surprised. There is no use to tell them anything for it makes bad worse." A letter Henry had recently sent home stating that no one could speak against the government or the abolitionists had made brother Fred and others quite angry. The most irritating thing about Copperheads, in Elise's opinion, was their sheer lack of fortitude. "You have no idea what great cowards the copperheads are. I think they would do the rebs very little good, if it came to fight. All they are good for is to slander." Elise concluded, "Your people think they are the best Christians in the world. It is true your Father prays, I believe much. But I can tell you if they are right, then you and I are wrong."[156]

CHAPTER 9

"THIS REBELLION MUST BE CRUSHED"

Christian penned a letter from Springfield, Missouri, describing a devastating raid by Confederate irregulars near Baxter Springs, Kansas. The Baxter Springs Massacre, as it came to be known, occurred on October 6 when Quantrill dispatched half of his force under David Poole to attack the Union post. Federal soldiers were holding off the Confederate attackers with the aid of a howitzer when General Blunt arrived with about one hundred men heading south to Fort Smith, Arkansas. Quantrill's men were wearing Federal uniforms, so Blunt mistakenly thought they were part of the garrison riding out to meet him. Quantrill's forces quickly gained the upper hand, and although many of the surprised Union men tried to surrender, Quantrill's raiders killed seventy of them, including Major Henry Curtis, son of Major General Samuel Curtis. Union casualties were estimated at more than one hundred, while Confederate casualties were probably fewer than five. This attack again infuriated Union officials and the soldiers who patrolled these areas. It was denounced as another brutal act of cowardice, similar to the Lawrence raid. When Union soldiers came into contact with purported bushwhackers or guerrillas, they generally shot on sight and rarely took prisoners. If any of the plunder from the Lawrence Massacre were found in a farmhouse, for example, no quarter was usually given by the investigating soldiers.[157]

Christian wrote that it "is a very sad state of affairs that the rebels got in on our rear. I think sufficient force is sent out after them from all directions to punish them severely for their depredation." He surmised that the raid on Baxter Springs was intended to make Union forces pull back "from our southern base; but thank God they can not accomplish it as easy as they expect it." Christian placed the blame for the debacle squarely on the shoulders of the commander of the Department of Missouri, Union major general John Schofield, labeling him a Copperhead. According to Christian, this kind of thing did not occur while the "radical" General Samuel Curtis "was commander of this Department, perfect safety & harmony reigned both in Missouri & Kansas." Christian hoped to have a new commander in the department soon, "and we want one who is not afraid to hurt rebels." Christian did not believe that military leaders in the West could afford to be on the defensive. Shortly after Christian's comments, Schofield was transferred to the East to serve with General William T. Sherman. As for his part, Christian suggested when the retribution against bushwhackers ought to occur. "The leaves will soon fall off of the trees & bushes and then where will there be a hiding place for Quantrill and his bloody gang."[158]

On October 19, Henry wrote a letter to Elise, thanking her for her concern and stating that Elise's letters helped him "forget the sufferings and hardships of a soldier's life." Henry believed that the most valuable thing civilians could do for a soldier was pray. God "will certainly not shut his heart against the supplications to the throne of Grace, of an old aged Father, a feeble Mother, or a tender Sister; indeed the prayers can accomplish much when they are sincere from the depth of the heart." When Henry endured "the highest precipice of the fever wrestling with death," or "while the bullets were flying around me by thousands," it was a great encouragement to know "that the supplications from my paternal roof were ascending to [the] throne of Grace, laying in petition to him who never refuses…. Prayers can accomplish great things!!" Henry ended this letter by mentioning other challenges that he faced in daily camp life. The first was sinful temptation, and he asked Elise to "pray for me that I may pass these temptations unmolested." Henry was also fighting to regain his health from a bout with diarrhea. He remarked that "it is a hard case for one to get right well again if he is broken down, but I concluded to submit to my fate patiently and hope to God if it is in his indefinite will, he may soon restore me to my former health."[159]

Elections took place in Ohio during the fall of 1863, and Elise took the opportunity to share the political climate of Holmes County with Christian. Campaign parades and rallies were held with the various candidates, and Elise recounted the traitorous and pro-Southern comments made by the Copperheads. It was especially galling with Union boys in the field. Elise remarked that when some of the abolitionists marched by, she wanted to wave her handkerchief but did not "for the sake of mother." Some of these political rallies turned violent, including one particularly long wagon caravan that paraded through the town of Millersburgh. Because they were pro-Union and against the Copperhead factions, they were stoned. Elise "contributed 25 cents toward a flag. I was not asked for it. It was even told me that it was not expected from a Soldier's Wife, but I was urged by a feeling of Patriotism." Elise informed Christian that he had "no idea how we are oppressed and lies told on us Union people, and the worst of it is, you dare not say a word at least, I dare not, I have tried with your folks and I can tell you that without the utmost necessity, I shall do so no more." Elise closed with a revealing, sentimental sketch of herself:

> *Let me tell you something that may perhaps please you Love. Could you take a peep in your boyhood home of an evening say sometimes at 9 or 10 o'clock, you might see a form of medium height and size glide up a flight of steps into a little room. The window of which looks out toward the East. That form is that of a woman yet young, but if you could look at her you would see that she is wrapt in deep thought. Sometimes, she will look grave, and sad, but often you would see a happy smile cover her face to which all sadness has to make room. But let us see what brings her to that place every night. She usually has a candle in her hand which she sets upon a board or shelf which serves instead of a table upon which she has a Testament and Hymn book ready for use. She is often weary of the days labor and toil, but arrives to her lonely appartement, she seems to have forgotten the days hardships, with a grateful heart to a kind Father in Heaven, that another day has come to an end. She picks up her Testament, reads a chap., then the Hymn book and some hymn's are also read. This done, you might see her kneel by the side of her couch, and if you could hear, it would be the low whisper of prayer to him who seeth even in secret; with silent tears trickling down her cheek's, she brings her petitions before the Lord. First for herself, then for a Loved One far away, then for all her friends and loved ones. For friend and foe and last of all, she agonizes for her country. And often she feels as if though the Lord would answer her prayer. Ere long after this, she arises, sits to her board and writes a letter to a friend; this done, she undresses herself, wispers a blessing upon herself and all her loved ones. In bed, she takes a paper from under her pillow and reads about half an hour, then she puts out her light and fals in sweet and refreshing slumber from which she awakes, with new strength in the morning.[160]*

Henry debated politics with Christian in a letter written in November 1863 from the Union camp on Folly Island, South Carolina. Henry had hoped that they could shelve the divisive topic for the duration of the war—"if we shall both live till then, we may speak about it then; as to my views they are unchanged yet, but shall that sever us?" Henry rhetorically asked if the subject of politics should "bring discord and lamentable consequences upon our family & relatives at home? Shall it be the cause and produce a deadly hatred? Shall it make brothers to bitter enemies? No! Never!" Henry acknowledged that he was still a Democrat but also a staunch "Union man." Henry movingly argued that would rather "be covered in a desolated sandy grave, within the limits of South Carolina unnoticed and unmourned, far, far away from home" before he witnessed the fall of the republic. Henry had been informed that because of the political tensions, Christian intended for Elise to return to St. Joseph. "Can you have an intention to remove her, and bring sorrow upon our dear old Parents heads, then I say you would have done by far better if you would never have sent her there. Contemplate over the matter in calmness before you act." While it remains unclear from existing letters precisely when Christian changed political parties, it is safe to assume that by this time he had informed his family that he was a Republican. Henry also implied that Christian was an abolitionist, a term Christian previously eschewed.[161]

The situation in Ohio was undoubtedly heating up, and Elise's letters of early November detailed some of the inner turmoil existing in the Isely household. First, she told Christian that she did not want to argue with members of his family. "You say that I ought not to be silent any longer and that you believe this to be a sin," but she explained that the few times she uttered some subtle criticism, she soon wished she had held her tongue. Elise related that almost everyone in the Isely family displayed some bitter feelings. The only exceptions were Christian's sister's kind husband and Fred's wife, Pauline, who "has been very kind to me." Elise added that the men of the household frightened her. "You know Dear that I am not naturaly man fearing, but I confess that there is something about your relatives here that makes me fear them. Never have I felt thus before, especially Father...he will not allow a word of his to be contradicted." Elise candidly stated, "Tis true, he reads his prayers, talks religion and much about being born again; but I got so far that I doubt that either of them all have experienced a change of heart." Elise cited scripture to support her argument. "If a man say, I love God, and hateth his brother, he is a liar: for he that loveth not his brother whom he hath seen, how can he love God whom he hath not seen." Elise explained to Christian that arguing with all of them was completely useless. "Pray how much do you think I could accomplish with people whose feelings are such as I faintly discribed above.... I do not mean that I do not, or will not, defend myself.... If I answer to one, they all pitch onto me."

Elise added that with regard to Christian, "they will not believe your word, although you speak facts that you have seen with your own eyes. I heard your father say that Abolitionists don't speak the truth." By plainly telling the truth, Elise "made both your Father and Fred swear so angry." Fred "has so little control over his temper that...he will fly into a passion and speak so angry and insulting that the one speaking to him finds him or herself in no enviable condition." Elise explained that she had not said anything against Fred or his party but simply declared that "this rebellion must be crushed, and that the rebels must be made to submit." Both of Christian's parents came to Fred's aid, and his mother used "the most insulting language" when arguing with Elise. Still, Elise was "blessed...with a calm and composed spirit" and pledged to remain cordial to Fred although she no longer respected him.[162]

Elise also informed Christian that she visited true Union people without the knowledge of the Iselys. Northern loyalists, including Pastor Bierrie and his family; John Kunzli and his family; and a few other church members were slandered by Christian's family and the other local Copperheads. Under the circumstances, Elise entreated Christian not to be too harsh or hasty. "It seems that not one of [them] thinks for himself, but they are the dupes of their leaders, what their papers say, that is so, and that they believe." She pleaded with Christian not to use harsh or sinful language, not to repay evil with evil. As for her part, Elise vowed to "reward all the evil done me, with good." She concluded her letter of November 6 by telling Christian, "It is more out of fear than anything else that the Copperheads opposed the Government. Out of fear that they will have to go into the army. They are great coward[s] and would do little good to rebs if it came to fight."[163]

Christian's life had become much more eventful in recent weeks. In a letter dated November 6, Christian related to Elise what the past ten days had been like. After a difficult but safe journey from Springfield, Missouri, to Fort Smith, Arkansas, Christian and his comrades received some bad news. It was reported that rebels infested the town and had taken prisoner many men who were out on scout or picket duty. "Poor Wm. Nelson had to be one of the number. Ten of them had went out on a scout on Saturday, they were ambushed, fired into and four of them cut off and taken prisoners." A scout of forty men went out to look for the missing men. The party found three dead, "brutally murdered" and stripped of all clothing. "Poor Nelson had several bullet holes and gashes in his head and body" and was "perfectly naked." The soldiers could do nothing for him "but build small rail pens around them to keep hogs from eating them."

The atrocities were committed by General Douglas Cooper and his Choctaw Indians, who along with other Confederate forces hoped to take back Fort Smith. Cooper, whose main supporters were the Choctaws and Chickasaws, concerned himself with the idea of recovering the fort, while Cherokee chief Stand Watie was primarily concerned with keeping Union troops out of Indian Territory. Christian wrote that the entire "[r]egiment was ordered to saddle up and be ready for a three days trip." They pursued the rebels, chasing them within six miles of their main camp. Christian wrote that the main body had evacuated the camp and that the only thing that occurred was the taking of some prisoners, mostly stragglers. On the way back to Fort Smith, the regiment came by the spot where Nelson's "body lay by the side of the road. I tell you it was a sad sight. Nelson was well thought of by all who knew him. He was an honest upright man, never swore, nor played cards." Christian remembered that the previous spring at Fort Scott, Nelson "wanted to give me some money to send it to you, to buy a present for the kindness you showed him when he was wounded in Leavenworth." Christian refused the gift and told Nelson that he and Elise had done "no more than our duty, he shed tears and thanked me." Nelson then told Christian of some narrow escapes that he and the regiment had survived. Nelson said, "Often have we been in such perilous conditions that the rebels could have killed every one of us and yet not a man was hurt, because the Lord is on our side." Christian concluded his letter on a more pleasant note. A few days after the sad death of Nelson, Christian and eleven other men were the escort under a rebel flag of truce for a prisoner exchange. During one evening, they camped "where an old German lives, a shoemaker. He told us many interesting adventures of his experiments and all in a laughing, happy mood. You better believe him and I done some tall laughing and Dutch talking and made the whole congregation Laugh. I tell you he talked Loyalty to one's hearts content."[164]

Even amid the conflict and the difficulties that arose, joyful moments occurred. As Christian had predicted during his time spent at Fort Leavenworth, he was happier in the field or on the move. He felt like he was doing something, and time passed more quickly. Of course, the potential for danger was higher, and seeing friends die certainly kept Christian anxious. The war was far from over, but in one of Elise's letters, she commented that the first snow would soon fall. She hoped that it would be the first snow of the last winter that they spent apart. The year 1864 was rapidly approaching, and Christian's three-year enlistment was set to expire near the close of that year. But that was too far in the future, for now the war had to be won, each day had to be lived and only faith in God and country provided the impetus for continuing the struggle.

As the end of November approached, Elise wrote a letter in which she once again talked about the political battles at home and how they had spilled over into the Isely family church. Pastor Bierrie was a loyal soul, yet he had to suppress his true feelings to the point of not even praying in church for soldiers. According to Elise, Christian's parents and brother Fred were as stubborn concerning religion as with politics. In her letter, she related the fear all loyal people shared regarding speaking or meeting openly. She concluded with a reference to their final parting and future reunion: "It is now 6 months since I came here. I can assure you that I feel thankful that they are in the past instead of being in the future. It is also past 8 months since our painful parting at the Depot in St. Joseph and I sometimes wonder how many more months it will take ere we shall be permitted to meet again, if we meet at all." Elise fervently prayed for the reunion. "I think of the many prayers that go to the Mercy Seat in your behalf which I think the Lord will be pleased to hear in mercy and spare us that we may live to see each other, live to the honor and Glory of his Holy Name."[165]

Winter was quickly approaching, but as Christian wrote his last letter in November from Dardanelle, Arkansas, he was still spending plenty of time in the saddle. Christian wrote that on one particular five-day scout in Scott County, they captured several notorious bushwhackers. Most were caught by the 2nd Kansas, "and if they were mean ones and known by the Mountain Feds were killed by them." At Dover, in Pope County, the regiment came upon a guerrilla band and had a "little fight." Christian wrote that "we took several prisoners. One of our men got badly hurt by his horse running against a tree, otherwise no one was harmed. We continued scouting through the Country all day." Amid all of this activity, Christian wrote to Elise that he thought often of her and was "in fact calm, resigned and happy, and in fact have been the largest portion, for a good while. I feel often just as happy as ever I did in my life. I know my dear Eliza prays much for me." Although this area of Arkansas had not been settled long, Christian stated that it was full of "rich and productive valleys, and the beautiful high, green mountains." However, he had seen many "fine and extensive cotton Plantations...all have been deserted having all been [burned by] rebels." The former slaves were destitute, especially "some old negros and negro children, such as are of little benifit at present, to their inhuman and ungrateful owners." Christian wrote that many of the people in the area were flocking to the "Stars & Stripes...to prove their loyalty by their deeds." In the Deep South, they had been "shut out from the light...the poor, deluded people of Dixie are kept in darkness and ignorance...every mail communication was broken up in the entire State in order to succeed better in keeping the people ignorant." Christian ended by saying, "If the southern Aristocracy had not used this shameful plan they could [not] have carried on the war as long as they have. But believe me when I tell you that such a conduct is already comming down with vengeance upon their hidious & fiendish schemes."[166]

About one week later, on December 5, Christian discussed an evening spent with some of the local Mountain Federals. A loyal mountain family invited Christian and his fellow "Bluecoats" to have breakfast. The father and eldest son wore Federal uniforms. "Maybe you think breakfast did not taste good where it was got up in such good style and where it came so free." Christian remarked that it was hard to imagine how much these loyal people of the mountains suffered because of their dedication to the cause. Later, Christian and his detachment came upon a home in the mountains. As they approached, the lady of the house, who looked "as pale as death, and acted and looked just like a person who has been caught in the act of a crime," appeared slowly in the front yard. The woman asked if the men were "Feds," and upon hearing that they were, said, "I am so glad. I have been in continual dread for the last few days." She told them that she had been weaving some cloth, and she was afraid that the "rebs would dash in before I could get it done; and take it from me. They take everything that they can lay their hands on. They took my last horse right from under me, and left me with my saddle on the road." Following the mother's appearance, a young girl of "about 14 summers came out of the woods from behind the house with her bare head and her white locks streaming promiscuously downward, and with a crimson flush and a look of confidence and smile upon her face." Christian wrote that she, too, asked if the soldiers wanted any of their clothes, to which Christian replied, "No, Lissie." Due to the fact we "did not take the clothe[s] from the poor half naked children...they were then convinced that we were not rebs." Christian next informed Elise that these people "cannot tell us from rebels" because "as many of the bushwhacking rebs as can, get the federal uniform...If they kill one of our men, or take one prisoner, they strip them of all their clothing."[167]

Christian wrote to Elise a week later with an interesting story of an old "Texican" who tried to join the Union forces. The man was almost hanged on a variety of occasions and his family persecuted, yet he was willing to fight for the Union. One of the Texan's sons went south a Copperhead and came back a Union man. Christian clearly admired the perseverance of these loyal Southerners. Christian also told Elise that he wrote a letter to John Kunzli back in Ohio, stating that if all loyal Union people had done their jobs before the war, the vile Copperheads would never have come into existence. In Christian's opinion, God was chastising Northerners for not being true, loyal patriots sooner. The most interesting part of the letter was a comment that Christian made to Elise regarding the importance of women on the homefront. "I am also well aware that if it was not for our dear loving patriotic women at home, that we could not carry on this war as successfully as we do and have done all along."[168]

Six days before Christmas, Christian wrote a letter in which he reiterated that the best weapon during these trying times "is that blessed priviledge, Prayer." Christian wrote that Elise stated, "There is charm in the little word, 'Love.' So there is...also quite a beautious charm in the blessed word, 'Prayer.'" Christian added that "I believe I have acquired a degree in Prayer... that I have never enjoyed before. God be praised." Another weapon that Christian used "against Satan" was "a good natured" disposition against even "the most perversed of men, and I also try to make myself at home wherever I am." Christian also employed "a feeling of tolerance towards all men.... concerning political views, I have also received a generous heart enough to make allowances there. My motto is: Extend charity and you will receive charity." This letter and its tone of confession and transformation undoubtedly pleased Elise, and it significantly delineated the differences between Christian and those who disagreed with them, both politically and militarily. In previous correspondence, Christian had at times seemed unforgiving or embittered, but in his letters of late December, he had come to the realization that his relatives were not likely to change their point of view, especially through argument. "My Savior had compassion when he seen me in my lost condition, and if I am different from what I have been, why the praise all belongs to my Divine Redeemer." Christian imagined Elise standing in front of him, saying "as only a tender, affectionate, loving wife is capable of saying: 'My Dear Christian,' Yes my 'Darling Eliza.'" However, he knew that much hazardous military service and many severe trials remained. "Therefore, let us be vigilant till our task is finished...that we may receive light & strength to enable us to discharge our duties well, till He in mercy brings about the happy issue which will surely grow out of it, if we are faithful."[169]

Christian not only faced temptation and Confederates, but his body was also fighting the effects of the December weather. Christian wrote that it had been very cold of late, making it almost impossible to compose a letter in a tent with near-numb hands. "I have nevertheless a warm heart left yet, which beats with emotion, prompted with most ardent and sanguine affections, for that dear One, that I am now attempting to address." In spite of the weather, Christian was sent on a scouting party that went over the battleground of the Devil's Backbone. As the men approached, they saw several graves, and on top of the mountain, Christian saw quite a few graves, "where the rebels had buried their dead." In a pretty area on "the banks of a little brook, a very nice round Mound with several trees standing on it," Christian found the solitary grave of "poor Wm. Statz…buried on top of the mound." The grave was enclosed, "and a board at his head is placed to show his Name, Company and Regiment to which he belonged. I was very much impressed with my dear friends place of Rest, but was pleased also when I found that such a nice place was selected for him."[170]

As 1863 came to an end, Elise wrote to Christian that she also anxiously awaited their reunion. She noted that while she had decided to not argue with the Isely family, that did not stop her from being offended by some of their remarks. One of her main complaints was against brother Henry, whom Elise described as "2 sided." How could "a man, who loves his country…be continually complaining," she wondered. According to Elise, Henry was "the Baby at home, yea, your Mother's Idol, and Father's pride; petted and cared for very tenderly." Elise felt that Henry was always defended and protected, while Christian was openly abused for his beliefs. Christian made a significant diary entry as the year 1864 dawned. He gave credit to God for his continued safe passage through the conflict and prayed to see the end of "this wicked rebellion, and the restoration of peace, and tranquility, and our Beloved Land once more United, Happy & Free. May I also be so unspeakably happy as to enjoy the close of the present year with her, who of all earthly things is most dear to me, even my own Darling Wife," as well as all those who are "near and dear to me, face to face."[171]

In January, Christian received a letter from longtime friend John Kunzli, who was disliked by the rest of the Isely family. Kunzli presented Christian with a drastically different view of the political climate in Holmes County. He wrote that even Henry supported Copperhead policies and should ask forgiveness for promoting the "cause of the government's enemies, by supporting the Vallandigham party, whom he can not help but know to be a traitor to our government." Kunzli's reference was to Clement L.

Vallandigham, an Ohio Democratic politician and passionate critic of Lincoln's policies. Vallandigham saw himself as a warrior for peace, but even some members of his own party "believed him devoid of patriotism and devoted to self-interest, playing a partisan fiddle while Rome burned." Vallandigham popularized the phrase, "The Constitution as it is, the Union as it was," which acquiesced to slavery. He appealed to many midwestern Democrats because he argued against the slaughter and opposed the abolition of slavery. Assuredly, Christian and the majority of Union supporters saw him as a traitor, aiding and abetting the Confederate cause, pushing political dissent beyond acceptable limits. Based on the statements that Kunzli made about Henry, a feud between the two of them had developed. It is difficult to discern Henry's true political sentiments. He claimed to Christian and Elise that he was a Democrat but supportive of the federal government and the Union cause. Unfortunately, no letters that he sent to others during this period are known. It is likely, though, that Henry's opinions lay somewhere between those of the strong Unionists and those who voiced their discontent. In Christian's view, however, there was no middle ground.[172]

Christian wrote a letter on January 11 from Waldron, Arkansas, noting that "the enemy was reported advancing, and every night, squads of our men had to go out on the different roads from 10 to 15 miles, out and see if they are approaching." His regiment had to stand picket on many roads, keeping up two "out posts about 40 men strong each." On December 29, "one of the outposts was attacked by a rebel force." Christian was on picket that night with three others when they "heard the shooting going on for quite a while." The rebels had run in on an outpost, "shooting and yelling, and demanded their surrender, but our gallant boys told the rebs. that there was none present of that 'name' and commenced plugging it into them and succeeded in killing their leader…and wounded a good many. They killed 2 of our Boys, and wounded 6 or 7 and after their leader was killed, they made a hasty retreat." The next few days were difficult for the regiment because it lacked decent provisions. Christian wrote that following New Year's morning, "we had nothing to eat, save a little corn bread, lean pork, and corn meal coffee. Such has been our fare for several days and [we] were very glad to get that much." Another significant event that occurred in early January was the opportunity for reenlistment. Christian was encouraged by many of his friends to reenlist in the "new enterprise…. I thought I would first serve my old time out before I contract for more." This meant that Christian's three-year term of service would expire in October 1864. The prospects were bright that he would see Elise before the year ended. Christian also believed

Clement L. Vallandigham, Ohio Democrat politician. *Courtesy Library of Congress.*

that the war would end in 1864, "every thing has a tendency towards a speedy over throw of the gigantic conspiracy." Moreover, Christian believed that more people were realizing how able President Lincoln was a chief executive. "The people…begin to see more clearly that Mr. Lincoln is the right MAN in the right PLACE."[173]

On January 15, Elise composed a most forthright letter to Christian, giving clear evidence that she was not afraid to challenge her husband's principles or opinions. She had a strong sense of what was proper and right, and while her views usually were shared by Christian, occasionally they differed, and at times Elise articulated her displeasure. She wrote that she was happy that Christian had changed his mind concerning his parents. "It has long been my heart's desire that you would not be so hasty and rash. Do not be offended at my calling you rash, for such you have been, for I must say that you have often made my heart throb with anxiety when you threatened to write them." Elise chided her husband that he sometimes went "a little too far," but she added that "you did not mean any harm and it seems to me that then you could not comprehend the state of things and the feelings of the people here." In a later letter, Elise acknowledged that Christian differed greatly from his family. "May God ever preserve me from their wrath…for I must say my Darling that if you were that way, I could not be your Wife. My nature is such, it wants to be treated with affection and since it has pleased the Lord to change my heart," it was often painful to hear "uncharitable and unfeeling remarks about my fellow man and this I can assure you I often have to hear."[174]

In late January, Henry decided to defend himself directly to Christian. Addressing the subjects of allegiance and commitment, Henry argued that people of Christian's political persuasion see only two groups: abolitionists or "rebel sympathizers." Henry told Christian that if he could not restrain himself from this type of "fanaticism…you would not want to meddle with a Traitor, nor read his letters, and unwillfully our correspondence would be suspended forever." Henry maintained that while he might "fight, bleed and even die on the battle field for my and your country…you classify me in sentiments amongst those fire-eaters, rebels and arch Traitors of Rebeldom against whom I have been battling for more than fifteen months." Henry explained to Christian that he did not shrink from duty when he marched up to the mouth of the cannons or when men were killed to his right and left. Henry contended that both parties went to extremes, and Christian, by "denouncing the vicinity of Winesberg as a 'black secesh hole,'…made my own blood recoil." Acting as a peacemaker, Henry explained that if both sides toned down their rhetoric, familial ties would surely improve. Henry somberly noted that if one of them were killed during the conflict, they would never meet again. "My affection to you shall never cease and should it be my fate to yield up my insignificant life on the battlefield, before and amidst of the roaring of the enemies cannons, my last and fervent desire shall be to meet you as a loving brother beyond the grave." Henry entreated Christian to "pause, and contemplate" that "peace and harmony will soon

The Military Campaigns of Christian Isely

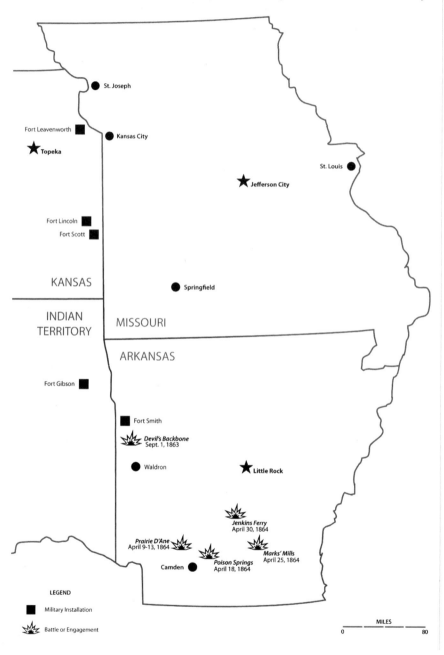

The military campaigns of Christian Isely. *Map by Matt Walker.*

be reestablished...I will try to soothe those at home too, if it is in my power to do."[175]

Despite the unpredictable vagaries of the battlefield, Henry and Christian hoped that the end of the war was coming and that the Isely family would be reunited. Experience was proving to be a great teacher to Christian, and as his third year of service began, he was a veteran adept in the art of survival.

Chapter 10

"LINCOLN IS THE SOLDIER'S CHOICE"

E lise once wrote at the beginning of the war that her only regret was that she was not a man, so she could not join the fight herself. Her dedication to the Union was complete, but by early 1864, she was tired of the burdens of the war that she had personally suffered. She felt thankful that Christian had not reenlisted. "You know I love our cause dearly, but it would almost have broken my heart to think that I should wait so long again before seeing you." Elise wrote that she could not endure another few years like the previous two, bowing to everyone's whims and keeping silent when she disagreed. "Yes, I firmly believe that the very hairs of my head would turn gray, and my forehead wrinkeld, and I would be a wreck of my former self. No one knows or has an idea what I had to go through." Elise recounted the high cost paid by her family. "My darling Bro. Adolphe laid down his life at the Altar of our Land. And may I not add yet that in consequence of my troubles it cost the life of our Darling Baby. And many a silent tear I have shed for our gallant Braves. My daily petitions also ascend the throne of Grace in their behalf." Elise prayed that God would spare Christian's life, and although she was "quite willing to assist in doing something for my Country, but I cannot say that I am willing to give you up again unless I could accompany you wherever you went."[176]

Elise commented on several occasions that she tried to cultivate the friendship of Unionists rather than the Copperheads, but because of the feelings of the Isely family, this was quite difficult. One individual she continued to come into contact with was the fiercely loyal Mrs. Bucher, who worked as the postmistress "to release a man for the battlefields. Her father, a man of sixty years, was in the army, so were her two…sons, one a mere boy of sixteen." Bucher encouraged her young sons to "serve their country valiantly." Elise wrote that the boys "did do their best…in fact the sixteen-year old boy was killed in battle. I was at the post office when the news arrived telling of his death. Tears streamed down Mrs. Bucher's cheeks until they wet the letters she was sorting; but she declared that if her twelve-year old son were old enough, he too should go to work the gun of his fallen brother." Elise related another story about how families dealt with the deaths of their loved ones. While soldiers were usually buried where they fell, Elise wrote that "funerals were held for them at home. With bowed heads unionists and disloyalists alike received the news of the death of their sons, for the sons of the disloyal were in the army too." Whether they were drafted or "ran away to volunteer against the wishes of their fathers," many such young boys served. "At funerals for the dead soldiers, the home guards turned out to fire salutes over the graves, sons of the Copperheads as well as sons of the loyalists being given these honors."[177]

Elise composed a lengthy letter on February 14, complaining that there were many things she needed to discuss face to face with Christian and wondering when that would be possible. One positive outcome of her time spent in Ohio was that she viewed her own father and stepmother in a whole new light. "I shall appreciate my poor old Father's love and kindness more than I have heretofore. I used to think my Father a rude and somewhat unfeeling man, but I shall never think so again." In a similar vein, regardless of the difficulties in Ohio, it was essential that she and Christian were kind to his parents, especially his mother. At the prospect that Christian would not visit Ohio after the war, "this made Mother very sad for she desires to see you, and have you come here very much. And now my Love it is not my design to dictate to you, but I believe it is your duty to come." Elise explained that not coming to see his parents could have long-lasting effects on the family. "To honor Father and Mother is our duty as children and Christian[s] besides it is the only commandment which has a promise for this world…. if I was old, and one of my children would refuse to come and see me, perhaps for the last time on earth, I believe it would almost break my heart."[178]

Christian wrote his next few letters from Waldron, Arkansas, where the troops were experiencing a brief respite. Recent scouting expeditions had been relatively uneventful, except for the capture of a few rebels. One night during a campfire discussion, the prisoners were seated around the Union men. Christian wrote that the evening "was spent in talking good sound

Union Doctrine. The prisoners were very attentive listeners—I...made myself also very busy in being kind to the prisoners...they did not expect such kind treatment of us." Christian's letter of February 18 dealt primarily with the subject of reenlistment. He explained to Elise that she should not be anxious about the matter, even though about half of his company reenlisted. To Elise's added relief, Christian revealed his plans to visit Ohio after the expiration of his current enlistment, in part because his carpentry skills were sorely needed at the Isely home. Christian concluded his letter with some advice for Elise. "I never was dissatisfied with you.... There is only one thing in which I blame you slightly." Apparently, at one point, Christian's mother claimed that he stated Elise's design was to "make infidels out of them." Christian responded that Elise should have told her to "[s]how me the letter...be a little more prudent when they come with such stuff.... But I will not command you much hereafter, you must be your own judge." Christian apologized if his "advising cause you distress.... I done the best I knew, under present circumstances." A contrite Christian concluded by saying, "[P]er chance you get along better without my advice," and hoped that Elise would "not cease to be satisfied with her humble Christian, notwithstanding his many faults."[179]

Christian wrote a week later from near Jenny Lind, Arkansas, following the Union evacuation of "that old rusty place, Waldron." Christian wrote that as they prepared to move out, there was "glee and joy" in the entire camp. "Big fires were made—and patriotic warsongs were sung, till the dark midnight hours, and commenced again next morning long before daylight." Everything that the Union soldiers could not take with them "was turned over to the flames." Christian added that as they left Waldron, he "never witnessed a more jubilant affair" in his life. The city was reduced to ashes; Christian saw the smoke ascending from a distance of fifteen miles. Christian reflected on the many scouts he had participated in the past few months. "I must acknowledge that I had often anxious thoughts concerning the safety of my life, when out on dangerous scouts, but I feel often even more alarmed about my poor Eliza, than about myself when [I] think that you might die with grief, sadness and for want of sympathy." Christian confided to his diary in late February that he wished he could sway his family's lack of charity. He regretted that his "poor Wife has still to be a victim to their narrow minds. May the Lord enlighten them."[180]

The Isely family got a welcome surprise in the last week of February. It had been reported that members of the 67th Ohio, Company C, were scheduled to receive a furlough. Henry was a member of that unit, yet he made no mention in any of his letters about the possibility of coming home. When the men began to arrive, however, Henry was among them. Elise wrote to Christian on February 27, describing the scene and her impressions of Christian's youngest brother. "It was a great joy for Mother. I was also glad to see Bro. Henry; but when I see a soldier, it always awakens a strong desire within me to see my Darling Christian." Henry was not well when he arrived, having "taken a very bad cold which had settled in his throat, but by good care and nursing he got soon well again." Elise described Henry as "very stout and hearty. He is also a very handsome and amiable young man. I might yet add with winning and pleasant manners." Now, having met Henry in person, Elise declared that "he is not so extreme like the rest of your folks." In fact, Henry showed no sympathy for rebels, "but in the contrary he puts them in their true light and tells what they are…. he is more of a patriot that I had taken him to be by his letters to his folks." Elise ended by remarking that in spite of the fact that Henry was a person of high quality, "I have not found a person that I could compare with…my Christian."[181]

Christian wrote a letter at the end of February, following a reconnaissance to Backbone Mountain. As he stood his lonely guard, he contemplated his military career. He first noted that it was the second anniversary of the death of his brother-in-law, Adolph Dubach. He next remembered his good friend William Staatz, who died six months earlier "near the very spot we stood picket." Lastly, Christian's reflections were triggered by the fact that while on picket they "found the bones of a man, and his half rotten rebel uniform all scattered about in the brush." All of this filled him with "solemnity on that day, and the night following." Christian wondered if he "was still spared, [as] a living monument of God's mercy?"[182]

In a letter dated March 1, Christian discussed the possibility of being mustered out in May and making a visit to his parents' home in Ohio. He added that "if they do not like me, why then I need but make my visit very brief." Christian reasoned, "If I don't go, it will cause a great many misgivings and heartburnings, and a great deal of blame might even be laid upon my dear Eliza's head." He stated it was rumored that they would soon march to Fort Gibson in the "Cherokee Country." Christian also related that the next day "there will [be] 2 men shot here, a member of Co. 'E' 2nd R.K.V. [Regiment Kansas Volunteers], he is guilty of desertion, and conveying information to the rebels, and also of bushwhacking." Christian did not relate the crime of the second individual. A letter written a week later gave details of an expedition conducted in the vicinity of Caddo Gap to intercept a "rebel scout" that was making its way south. They arrived too late, after the enemy troops had proceeded through the gap. The following evening, while it rained and stormed, Christian and his detachment were attacked in camp. "We had quite a brisk shooting affair for a little while on both sides and although bullets flew pretty thickly yet only one of our boys of Co. 'D' was wounded. The rebels retired before daylight across the mountain."[183]

Refugees continued to pour into Union camps. Many were Texans, "seeking refuge beneath the flag they so dearly love." According to Christian, some of the refugees were harassed by Choctaw Indians. One of the groups that Christian came into contact with hailed originally from Missouri. The men reported that there was no end to the sufferings they endured "for their loyalty" and that it "is even getting worse every day. They say that Quantrill and his band of cutthroats is killing all that are not bowing their knees to Baal or the behests of treason." Christian wrote that the loyalists were liable to be conscripted at any age, and those who "utter a word against the rotten confederacy" were told that if they do not like the "Confederacy, then why don't you get out of it." When these Union men try to "make their way [out] of the land of oppression, then they are waylaid, bushwhacked, robbed, killed, and who knows what else of mean things is not done to those sadly distressed people at the hands of the slavery advocating rebels." Yet the "copperhead Democracy would go into a compromise with such fiends."[184]

Christian wrote a letter on March 12 stating that much of what Elise wrote suited him remarkably well, but he included several admonitions. One of Elise's shortcomings was her sensitivity, which led her to find fault with many people. "If persons don't suit you exactly, you soon discover their faults, and if they suit you, why then you are equally ready to cover up their faults…this may be right & proper, but still it shows to[o] much partiallity." For example, Elise was often too hard on Henry, who always wrote about her in the highest terms. Elise by this time had changed her opinion about Henry, acknowledging that he was a "praise worth[y] young man and people let him know so too."[185]

As the month of March came to a close, Henry's furlough ended. During his last evening at home, "nearly 40 persons ate supper here." Elise wrote that she could "not help feeling somewhat sad all the time." The following day, as many returning soldiers gathered to leave, Elise was determined to not shed a tear, but her heart "was soon moved when I saw our brave boys in blue, and when I thought that the parting moments had come for many, and also for our dear Henry, all this recalled past and bitter parting scenes to my mind." The scene brought to Elise's mind thoughts of Christian and "my darling Bro. Adolphe, of our darling Baby, of friends and home, and I also found it hard to part with dear Bro. Henry who has grown dear to me for many of his good qualities." Elise wrote that she wondered how to respond. Christian's family was rarely affectionate, and so Elise had decided to be subtle in her goodbye. However, after witnessing both his mother and sister show affection toward Henry, "I gave him one hand, the other arm I put around his neck and kissed him affectionately as I would have done by own dear Brother. He also quite affectionately kissed me. I also saw tears trickle down his browned cheek, which was done by the sun of S.C." After Henry got in a buggy, he "wiped his tears," shook hands with everyone again and told them to be of "good cheer." As the buggy pulled away, he "waved his cap" and called out, "I hope [we'll] meet again." Elise responded by waving her handkerchief. The regiment was off to Cleveland to "await orders." The entire episode caused Elise to tell Christian, "I too desire your return with a longing heart."[186]

On March 26, Henry wrote a letter to Christian from the camp at Cleveland. He detailed his visit home and informed Christian that Winesburg was not the "dark secesh hole" that Christian had been led to believe. Henry confided that Elise treated him "in such a way that no sister can surpass. Indeed, I think you have got a partner for life which seeks its equal, may you return safe and live many a happy day with her. That is my fervent wish and prayer." Henry shared with Christian that the 67th Ohio was a veteran regiment and that he had reenlisted; it was "under these conditions we were furloughed." Henry "was a single man and could be in the field better than many others and that is what induced me to put down my name. We go into the field with the intention to go and finish the rebellion. Many may fall yet. I may be one of them myself. If I do fall, I may have the satisfaction, that I tried to help to safe [save] our bleeding country." Elise wrote that Henry was certainly not a Copperhead—"he is too upright and truthful for that." If Henry had a weakness, it was that he might fall prey to flattery. Elise added that Henry was not as spiritually fit as Christian—"religion is to him, something gloomy and dry."[187]

Christian corresponded little during the month of April. On May 3, he explained to Elise that his unit had been on the move much during the preceding weeks. He wrote from the "Camp of the 3rd Brigade, 1st Division, Army of the Frontier," at Little Rock, Arkansas, giving details of their time in the saddle. His unit left its camp on March 28 and traveled through Danville, Hot Springs, Rockport, Arkadelphia, Spoonville and Okalona. On

April 10, Christian's regiment joined with General Frederick Steele's army. Steele—a veteran of Wilson's Creek, Pea Ridge and Vicksburg—was the commander of the Department of Arkansas. "Steele's Army moved out 8 miles & engaged the enemy on Prairie de Anne," driving them across three miles of prairie. The next few days were spent with "the exchange shots of skirmishes & the exchange shots of some artillery." On April 13, the army "started for Camden," located on the Washita River, and was attacked in the rear about noon. "The engagement soon became general. Our Reg. was deployd as skirmishers & flankers. None of us were hurt. The 1st & 2nd Ark. Inft. however had several killed by the rebel artillery, but we done them much more damage then they did to us."

Three days later, the division entered Camden, "a pretty large town & well fortified…. But at Camden, one misfortune after another befell us." On the seventeenth, "a forage train was sent out of 180 teams wagons & all, 4 pieces of artillery & about 1,000 men." A day later, the forage train was attacked by a rebel force of 7,000. "Our men fought bravely for about 4 hours, beating the rebels on every side. The Infantry engage[d] was some of the 1st Kan. Colored & 18th Iowa. The former lost 113 & the latter 70 in killed & missing. There were 9 there out of our Co., 4 missing…. Our whole loss there was about 225. The rebels loss is estimated much higher." Christian added, "Our boys were ordered with terrible oaths to surrender, which they promply refused to do & fought desperately as long as they could, then cut their way out." A short time later, a supply train "was captured along with 1300 men, including all of our mail." With that loss, Christian wrote, "it became necessary to evacuate Camden. The enemy pressed us on every side." On April 29, at the Saline River, the rebels struck at the Union rear again. Christian wrote that the "[c]av. forces did not participate in the fight, but we were out as flankers & soon as it was all over we were hurried to this Place to reinforce it." After arriving safely at Little Rock, Christian ended his letter by saying that all were in good spirits, despite the tension, and that if the rebels attacked them again, "we are ready."[188]

The 2nd Kansas Cavalry lost only a handful of men in all the skirmishing and light engagements during the month of April at Danville, Roseville and Camden. The larger action mentioned by Christian involving the 1st Kansas Colored and the 18th Iowa Regiment was the Battle of Poison Springs. Casualties at Poison Springs were about 300 for the Union and 114 for the Confederates. One of the main reasons for the higher Union casualties was that most of its wounded and captured soldiers were killed. In fact, the 1st Kansas Colored alone sustained 117 killed and 65 wounded. Christian did not mention being directly engaged, although the adjutant general of Kansas officially reported that the casualties of the 2nd Kansas at Poison Springs on April 18 were 2 killed, 1 wounded, 13 prisoners of war and 1 reported missing. The reference to the attack by Confederates on the Union rear at the Saline River is a reference to the Battle of Jenkins Ferry in Grant County, Arkansas. On April 30, Confederate forces attacked repeatedly, but the Union repulsed the attacks, and Confederate general E. Kirby Smith missed an opportunity to capitalize on the earlier victories at Poison Springs and Marks' Mills. Christian obviously had a busy April campaign. He wrote on May 5 that "the fatigues of our unhappy campaign...over come me." He also commented disparagingly on General Steele. "The whole army is very indignant about him. 'He is a Concervative, or Copperhead and is affraid of hunting the rebels' much is the cry of nearly all that I have heard yet." Such commanders cause "more harm than the open enemy in the field."[189]

When Elise finally received a letter from Christian in May, she breathed a sigh of relief; she was accustomed to hearing from him every week to ten days. She wrote that she "went to a secret place and poured out my heart into thanks and praises to God for his tender care and loving mercy toward us; we surely do not deserve it that the Lord should thus deal kindly with us." Elise added, "When I think of the many braves that have fallen and that my dear Christian has been spared thus, it seems to me that I cannot thank God enough for his loving care." Christian's entire family rejoiced at the news, although Elise reported that Christian's parents had been very low of late. Father was "weaker than he ever was since I am here.... Mother...breathes so short and gets harder hearing than ever so you see I am constantly with sick people." In a postscript, Elise noted that she had written on May 3, Christian's thirty-sixth birthday. At that time, she had not heard from him in five weeks, and she wondered if he was among the living or dead. Elise wrote that she was sad and lonely and expressed her feelings in sentimental poetry:

> *The moon that proudly treads the sky,*
> *Were doubly sweet if thou were nigh;*
> *The breeze that murmurs on mine ear,*
> *Were softer still if thou wert here.*
> *The sky would beam a lovelier blue,*
> *If thou could'st whisper, "I am true."*
> *And thoughts of heaven bear firmer away,*
> *If thou should'st point and head the way.*

She hoped "that the time is not far distant when we shall be permitted to see each other again from face to face. I must close wishing that I could give you a good night kiss." She then quoted a familiar verse of scripture: "I can do all things through Christ which strengtheneth me." Christian and Elise attempted to live by that philosophy, which they embraced even more resolutely in the most difficult of times.[190]

Christian wrote a letter to Elise on May 18 from a camp on Rector's Prairie, near Fort Smith. He recounted some of the military reverses of late and the increasing work on fortifications. "A large rebel force is reported between here & Little Rock under [John] Marmaduke, [Joseph] Shelby and others.... the rebel army is up here in [force] and...they will probably attempt to dislodge us from this our position. That however would be a very silly attempt as we are plenty strong enough to fight any army." Christian observed that it would be "folly at the present moment to scatter our Division to hold minor Posts." April had been filled with battles in and around Camden, Arkansas. The original intent of Union general Frederick Steele and his command was to march from their base at Little Rock, link up with General Nathaniel Banks and capture Shreveport. This became more difficult because of the stiff resistance offered by Confederate generals Kirby Smith, Sterling Price and Jo Shelby. The Union forces also lacked adequate forage and provisions in southern Arkansas. Steele decided, under these conditions, to change the direction of his march from Shreveport to Camden. So, as Christian penned his letters in early May, he was irritated with the reverses, as well as concerned over what might occur.[191]

Christian resumed his attack on the poor leadership of General Steele. While many rumors were afloat, Christian wrote that "the army here is in good spirits & sanguine of success, having complete confidence in our brave & patriotic commander, Gen. [John] Thayer." Christian added that if Steele had the "pluck & patriotism" of Thayer, we "would have give the rebs. such a complete flaxing down south on Prairie d'Anne, that they would not have bothered us again very soon and...Camden could be in our possession still." Steele's action in the recent campaign was described as "total mismanagement." Christian ended his letter of May 18 by discussing his chances of being mustered out of the service. He had once hoped that he would be mustered out in early 1864. That now seemed improbable, so Christian set his sights on October, only five months away. He encouraged Elise to be strong and to pray that Christian "might be out of the service in 6 more months and be with my Love. But then I do just as much almost desire that the war was over by that time and our dear Land and Country,

'Happy' and 'Free'!" Christian added that food was sometimes scarce of late. In camp, "we always have plenty to eat…but on a march we are often deprived even of a cup of Coffee. But it is all for this happy land of Canaan." Elise recalled many years later that the hardships of campaigning "were somewhat mitigated by a sense of humor which usually aids humankind in hours of difficulty." She remembered Christian telling of one day during the lean times, when "rations were limited to half an ear of corn each, the men took turns describing the grandest dinners of their lives, and at the end voted on what they would like to have to eat. Fried mush received the highest vote." On another occasion, when the only water they had was so saturated with "white soapstone that it colored the coffee," the men "smacked their lips and said they had cream in their coffee"; also, the hardtack was once so wormy that the men gave "three cheers for Andrew Jackson, on the theory that the hardtack was left over from the Battle of New Orleans. Shaking out the worms, they ate every crumb with relish."[192]

In the last week of May, Elise recounted a morning during which Christian and her father's home in Willow Dale dominated her thoughts. After her morning's work, Elise decided to take "a little ramble in the garden," gathering various flowers, including some roses, which made her "think of my Darling Christian." She plaited a few of the flowers into her hair and pinned one on her dress. She added, "I suppose my Christian will smile here and say what then Dear makes this so important. Well, just let me tell you." Elise reminded Christian of the time he worked at her father's house in "our sweet Willow Dale where for the first time a feeling of Love was awakened in my heart for you." While there, Christian often went to the Missouri River with her brother and retrieved flowers, especially roses. "One time you brought me some…and I trained some in my hair and the rest I pinned about my person. This seemed to please you very much for you looked upon me smilingly and you repeated a very pretty German verse about roses, the words of which I cannot now remember, but the circumstances I can never forget." Elise wrote that the entire episode prompted her to wonder where Christian was spending his "Sabbath morning." Elise wrote her next letter to Christian on June 6. "Never have you had so much worth in my eyes as you have now and although I often miss you sadly and long to have you near me, I feel nevertheless satisfied that you should stay until next Fall." She proudly added, "Never has our dear Union cause been so dear to me as it is now and I am glad that my Christian is able to lend a helping hand in putting down this wicket rebellion." Although Elise had not undergone the difficult military hardships that Christian experienced, she still "felt the meanness of rebels severely." She did not elaborate on this comment. Elise mentioned that one of Henry's close friends in the 67th Ohio died and that they held a funeral service for him. Based on Elise's letters from this period, it seems that some of the heated political differences among the Isely family had waned a bit.[193]

On June 10, Christian wrote from his new camp at Clarksville, Arkansas. Once again, they had been on the move, having left Fort Smith on May 20. The 2nd Kansas arrived at Clarksville on the twenty-second and realized that the town was held by rebels, "with Shelby close at hand." Colonel Cloud decided to push forward, "and as we got close to town the rebs got wind of it and skedaddled towards Shelby's command which was reported on big Piney only 10 miles off with 2000 men and 6 pieces of artillery, and there were only about 300 of us and no artillery." With Cloud in command, the Union troops were not in the least alarmed, and the regiment took up a defensive position, expecting an attack. On the following morning, Cloud "saw that they were not going to come," and so "he ordered that we should all dis-charge our arms, carbines & revolvers, which made a terrible crash...and undoubtedly scared the rebs if any were near.... this is one of Cloud's own peculiar tricks to play on the rebs." Elise wrote later that Cloud was "much beloved by his men.... He wore his hair in a long mane down his shoulders." She added that his "prompt decisions in action got his men out of many a tight place." Elise's version of the episode near Clarksville related that Cloud rode into a pine forest, not realizing that he was being followed by a large force. Cloud subsequently deployed his men on a wide front and instructed each man to pretend to be a captain "while the colonel thundered orders." The "captains" repeated the commands "to their mythical companies, which were supposedly hidden in the edge of the forest." Cloud's commands indicated that an entire regiment was about to go into battle, and the befuddled "Confederates skedaddled." Elise believed that "Colonel Cloud learned his strategy from Gideon, for he was a Bible-reading colonel, who taught his men to discard profanity no matter how hard was their situation."[194]

Henry wrote to Christian from a camp near City Point, Virginia, on June 16, again defending his political beliefs. Henry had written a letter published in the German-language newspaper *Westbote* that angered many, including Christian. John Kunzli mailed copies of the letter to the colonel of the 67th Ohio, among others. This appeared to be partisan politics carried to the extreme. Kunzli did this, Henry contended, because the colonel was "a man of their politic." Despite the fact that the colonel never said a word to Henry, this put Henry in a very uncomfortable position. Henry again stated that Christian's reference to Winesburg as a "dark secesh hole" was incorrect and hurtful. Henry's regiment had once again been in combat in the Bermuda Hundred Campaign. His unit participated in the Battle of Chester Station on May 10 and the Battle of Bermuda Hundred (or Ware Bottom Church) in Chesterfield County, Virginia, ten days later. Among the mortally wounded was Henry's "bosom comrad, tent and bunk mate since" he enlisted, Godfrey Hoerger. Henry explained that both sides had "fortifications from the James to the Appomattox river," as the Confederates under General Robert Ransom assaulted the Union force of General Benjamin F. Butler. The fighting was intense, and during the last engagement, Henry was at the front for two days and got "very little rest." He felt "dull and dizzy in my head, from the continual fireing. My hands are stiff, shoulder sore, also my mouth and teeth…as I shot some over 200 cartridges in these 3 days."[195]

Christian wrote a short letter on June 21 to Elise. It was her birthday, and Christian sent his blessings and told her how much she was in his prayers. He also discussed his family and the presidential campaign of 1864. Christian hoped that all "lovers of their Country," the "true patriots," would "vote for ABRAHAM LINCOLN in the coming contest. Lincoln is the Soldier's choice & favorite. This I only add by way of remark, and not for argument's sake." In early July, Christian sent home some of his letters, as well as his diary. He added that Elise need not worry about the meager fare on which he existed. Christian said that he was often more content with the "piece of hard-tack and a cup of black unsweetened coffee" than if he was "seated by a richly decked table with the good things so loaded down that it farely groans beneath its weight." He was richly blessed when compared with so many who "are crippled and maimed for life and those that are panting and suffering in a rebel dungeon or are stricken down with burning fevers." Christian took pride in his service to the Union because he could speak of the war with much more knowledge than those who never experienced it. Things around Clarksville had been routine, with the exception of the bushwhacking death of one scout named Scott Mayberry, a personal favorite of Colonel Cloud's. Christian concluded with a postscript dated July 4, writing, "We were awakened this morning by a Salute from our Artillery. May the very center of Jeff's Confederacy be shaken this day…and the whole Nation give praise and glory to God and pray Him to make us once more United and Happy."[196]

Christian wrote a few days later from Van Buren, Arkansas, where he was part of an escort for a forage train. The rumors were rampant. Some "say that the Regt. will not be mustered out, but each man discharged as his time expires." Others claimed that the entire regiment would be sent to Kansas "in the course of a few months to be mustered out, and…Col. Cloud is going to enlist a good Veteran Regt. out of the 2nd, 5th & 6th Kas. Cav." For his part, Christian was not troubled "with such unnecessary surmisings." He added that many people recently had sought the protection of the Union fort. "Old grey headed men and young boys go [to] their military Post for protiction, and during the harvest they went in flocks, with their cradles to cut their wheat." Christian wrote that one man stood guard with a gun against the attacks of bushwhackers while the others harvested the wheat. He rhetorically inquired, "Would this not be an excellent place for southern sympathizers? I think if any thing could cure their malady this would be a sure remedy." Christian noted that nothing in Arkansas was untouched by the war. Men of all ages were in some service, while women and children tried to maintain homes and farms. In addition, most farms and houses were "deserted and forsaken…and the fields are full of weeds and desolation. Such are affairs in Rebeldom!" Christian ended by stating that the rebels had contracted for such an ordeal, and "such they shall Have! Yes and such copperheads ought to have too."[197]

Christian composed a letter for Elise on August 6 from Fort Smith. The previous weeks had been occupied with preparations in the event of a feared Confederate attack. The only fighting that occurred during that time, however, involved isolated bushwhacking incidents, as well as a bit of firing by pickets, but most "were soon dispersed by a few well aimed shells." On August 3, Christian joined several others on a scout. After going across "the Prairie into the timber…we ran on to a squad of 5 in the act of robbing some distressed families." The men of the 2nd Kansas fired on the bushwhackers but got only one, "a very bad one at that. He had been in the bush for the last 2 years, and last winter when the deep snow fell, he enlisted in the 18th Iowa, stayed 2 months, stole revolvers, then went into the bush again." Christian simply stated, "One of our Co. shot him dead." Refugee trains often traveled through Fort Gibson to Fort Scott. Christian had requested to join the escort of a recent train, but his request was denied. Christian remarked that he was rarely "ahead" when favors were distributed, but in the few months that remained of his enlistment, "I shall ask no odds nor favors of Company Officials." Christian concluded by telling Elise that he did not expect to be stationed in one place much longer and that the regiment would return to Kansas soon, probably taking the road from Fort Gibson to Fort Scott. "I think also that it is the safest route for the next two months at least, as there are always soldiers marching on it escorting trains."[198]

A little less than two weeks later, Christian wrote again from Fort Smith, giving the latest particulars about bushwhacking incidents. A mail party from Fayetteville was attacked "something like 15 miles north of Van Buren, in a notorious place for the bushwhacking skulks." The estimated number of rebels was three hundred, while the Union escort consisted of sixty men of the "6th Kan. and other Regts." According to Christian, bushwhackers boasted that they had killed thirty men. If this were true, he calculated, they killed all who fell into their hands because there were only ten dead on the scene, while thirty made their escape by running for their lives. Christian suspected that the rebels killed the other twenty soldiers when they tried to surrender. In another incident, a mail party heading north was attacked in the Boston Mountains. Three members of the 2nd Kansas were killed and two wounded. One of the dead was Ed Norman, "a German and a good man." While all of this was disconcerting, and "the country north of us is full of prowling & thieving bushwhackers," Christian rightly surmised that such harassment would not change the outcome of the border conflict. He concluded his letter by stating that many of the men were heading to Kansas under Colonel Cloud and Major Henry Hopkins, and it was "said that the remainder of us will soon follow after." Christian added that some of the poorer Union generals were motivated by nothing but personal gain, and "many of them do not like Col. Cloud because he is so honest and upright."[199]

Henry began a letter to Christian on August 19 from Fort Dutton (formerly Fort Pride), near Point of Rocks, Virginia. After the first two paragraphs were completed, the 67th Ohio received marching orders. On September 9, Henry resumed his writing "before the ramparts of Petersburg in the midst of bombing cannons and exploding shells all around me." Henry graphically described the sights and sounds of the battle. The musket fire and artillery bombing were so commonplace, even at night, that "we don't mind it hardly anymore even if shells explode over our heads, they sometimes even throw shells more than a mile beyond in the rear of our camp." Although Henry witnessed quite a bit of combat during his term of service, "the front of Petersburg presents the biggest battlefield I ever have seen. The shattered trees bear testimony what horrible fighting has been done here already." The fact that Richmond was not yet in Union hands was not the fault of the Army of the Potomac. "The mistake must be looked for somewhere else and not in the soldiery." Henry ended his letter by asking Christian about the presidential election. "Do you go for Abe Lincoln to be our president for four years more? I tell you frankly, I don't; the great masses of the Potomac…go for their former commander, Gen. G.B. McClellan." Henry claimed that if McClellan had been reenforced during the Peninsular Campaign of 1862, he would have taken Richmond. "That's the common saying of all that were under him."[200]

In late August, Christian wrote to Elise that he had arrived in Fayetteville, despite a "serious difficulty." During the journey through an area "where bushwhackers were reported thick," some "of the 6th Kan. boys were beastly drunk." Their drunkenness prompted them to behave "shamefully," and they "abused some poor old citizens." The lieutenant in command "of the 14th Kansas, was so drunk that he did not know what he was doing. We then went to him and told him that we refuse to obey him. I told him that we will obey & follow an Officer as long as there is one of us left, but I refuse to obey Whiskey any further." The lieutenant "then yielded his command and a Sergeant of the 6th Kansas, a whole souled soldier, then took command, and we then disarmed the Lieut. and every thing went on quiet & successfully." When the lieutenant was sober again, the men allowed him to resume command. "And you better believe he has done first rate ever since. He is trying to do all he can for us and stays right in camp with us, sees that we get our rations, forage and our horses shod, and in fact has done better than any Lieut. or Capt. that I have ever been out with and is ashamed of his bad conduct." Christian praised the 1st Arkansas Cavalry for "keep[ing] the rebels low in this vicinity. I think more & more of them all the time…. Many of them have families here. Some of course have nothing but an humble tent, or even only a green shade tree for their shelter and but little to live on."[201]

On August 27, Christian wrote that he had decided after his term ended to come to Ohio and "embrace my sweet Eliza in my Boyhood home." Christian acknowledged that the "evil spirit has always suggest[ed] to me that I should never show my face there because they are treating my dear Eliza with such contempt," but he ultimately resolved "that I would come if my Life was spared, considering it a part of my Duty." He would be so full of "Singing & Laughing—if every thing goes as I trust to God that it may," his relatives would be ashamed to "pick a quarrel with me." He prayed that "we all live to the end of the war," when he would "try my utmost to make my aged parent[s] more happy and cheerful." Until that time, Christian wrote, let us "become truly willing cross bearers that we may be thoroughly fitted for all coming days," and "God deliver us from all troubles & calamities."[202]

The past two months had not been free of troubles for Christian. He was part of the guard on a few mail parties, which was always a source of anxiety, and the heat and provisions were difficult to bear. He had at times lacked for an appetite and suffered from headaches. Fortunately, during the summer, the Union troops lost few men to either the rebels or "scourching fevers." The worst appeared to be in the past. September approached with cooler temperatures and "a more gentle sway, bearing with it the choicest fruits, and then October with its forest clothed in purple hue." Christian was also bolstered by the fact that "our conquering Armies are advancing, and Dixie is declining, yes gradually dying.... And peaceful be the sway in all future days, of our beloved, of our beautiful flag of our Starry flag." Indeed, although the prospects of returning to Kansas seemed to be fading, Christian looked forward to being mustered out of the service and heading home.[203]

CHAPTER 11

"OUR MEETING"

Throughout the course of the Civil War, Christian shared his thoughts and opinions most fully in a letter he wrote on September 24 from Fort Smith. That letter represented the culmination of three years of war, as Christian vented his intense feelings about patriotism, loyalty and the causes for which the war was fought. He began by reflecting on everything that had transpired. He talked not only of his sacrifice but of Elise's as well. She left her "own little cottage in St. Joseph…to cast your lot among strangers in a strange land," undergoing many "dangers, hardships and privations." He wrote that she endured criticisms of her husband and country and had to listen to the "epithets from the lips of Southern sympathizers, who are living in the free and enlightened North and yet sympathize with Jeff. Davis and his slavewhipping, labordispising, truthhating Confederacy," which sought to overthrow our cherished "American Liberties and national Existence." Liberty-loving people were forced to respond to the South's suicidal plans and "hellish schemes which have their origin in the infernal region from the archtraitor himself, the avowed enemy and hater of true liberty and permanent human happiness."

Not only had Elise endured all of that—compounded by losses of a brother and a son and possibly a husband—she did it without even the ability to defend herself. "Not allowed freedom of speech in the free state of Ohio! When I think of such facts, my Dearest, I long to take my flight on eagles wings to hasten to your side to defend you." He added that she was "assailed and insulted" by the speeches and words of Clement Vallandigham, "the

Judas, who would betray his country to obtain power and assist Jeff Davis to destroy the Union, to gain his object." No such Copperheads had words of encouragement for "warworn veterans who fought so bravely for the honor of our and our Father's flag." They offered "no laudation for the unflinching integrity of Abraham Lincoln, who is making such energetic efforts to preserve and perpetuate the Union against all her enemies."

Christian assured Elise that although he was unable to "offer you my supporting arm," he had shed tears and prayed for her and was writing this letter as a "small tribute of gratitude" to Elise for her firm belief to "'Trust in God' under all circumstances." Christian then encapsulated his views on the "all important question of the times":

> *There are persons who would snear at, and condemn my sentiments; but I thank God, although such would uphold slavery and fetter the mind, I am not their slave yet. I do not want their favors. I care not for their frowns, but will do my duty to my God and my country, regardless of their secret midnight meetings, their conspirings against us, to contemplate our overthrow. Of my work, I am not ashamed, nor afraid to do it in open daylight, because it is the work of humanity, justice and right.*

The day would come when Copperheads wished that they had supported the Union unconditionally, and their "posterity need not be ashamed...by the black stigma which will mark everywhere the rebel sympathizer."

The next part of Christian's long letter sketched his political transformation. He retold how he went west to seek his own way in life and become a "good Democrat." Since May 1854, he had "been in the famous Missouri Valley, either in Missouri, Kansas, Iowa or Nebraska, and have been a watchful observer, and am personally acquainted with not a few of the bloody outrages perpetuated upon the honest, industrious squatter." Such a homesteader, according to Christian, came to Kansas "to establish a home, and by the sweat of his brow earn his living—he had of course no wooly head to bow to him at his bidding—believing the young Territory would enter the Union as a Free State, not only free from slavery but free for every american citizen to choose a home from the public lands." To Christian's surprise, some of the proslavery men who called themselves "good Democrat[s] said to me when I expressed my desire to take a claim in Kansas: 'We do not allow persons from free States to settle there...to fill the Territory with abolition doctrine.'" These proslavery men were determined to make a "Slave State out of it, even if it requires the force of arms to accomplish it." Still, Christian wrote, he clung to the name Democrat through the presidential election of 1860, supporting Stephen A. Douglas.

Christian's political transformation occurred in 1861, when some people began to place party over country and blamed Lincoln for the problems that besieged the government. Christian asked, "Whose fault is it then that today the war is not successfully and honorably closed and that the shedding of blood is not yet stopped? It is perfectly clear to all who love <u>light</u>, rather than <u>darkness</u>." Clearly, the rebels had known for the past two years their only hope was that Southern sympathizers in the North "would rise en masse against the Government, and help them slay its brave defenders, thus giving them ample time to establish their Confederacy, whilst we would be plunged into ruin and disgrace." It would be better for these sympathizers to live under the "jurisdiction of Jeff. Davis."

Christian illustrated his point by recounting acts of lawlessness in the South that he witnessed, as well as the difficulty loyal Southerners faced in trying to support the Union—all of this while Copperheads and Confederates alleged that Lincoln destroyed their freedom of speech. While Lincoln was thus abused and slandered, "nobody interferes with them" or tried to silence them except through reasonable debate. Christian added that what many Northerners were not aware of was the desire of the "southern oligarchs" to guarantee "State's Rights and their <u>divine Institution</u>, <u>slavery</u>.... It unavoidably behooves us then to extinguish every spark of the rebellious element." Referring to the symbol of Copperheadism, Christian added that in the North, "we bruise the serpents head by ballot, while in the South, we must pelt the hydra headed monster with bullet, shot and shell...till it lies lifeless in the dust." Christian reflected over the loss of life that he had witnessed and pledged his own life on the altar of freedom:

> *O my poor bleeding and distracted Land, many and various are thine ungrateful enemies; but to me thou art dearest of all others; should my friends forsake and betray thee, yet never could I cease to love thee. For thee, and the <u>flag of thy braves</u>, I have shed many burning tears, and offered my fervent prayers to God; for thee I forsook my sweet home and darling friends, and now sacrificed my health, and take my last resting place on one of Arkansas' rocky hills beneath the branches of a lonely oak or pine tree, far from home and loved ones, unnoticed and unwept for—<u>only may I never see the Sun of thy Glory go down, nor thy beautiful Union severed</u>.*

Christian prayed for Abraham Lincoln and thanked God that the president held true to the "helm of Columbia's precious bark to direct her through the storm and angry waves." Lincoln was not governed by "mere human speculation," but looking up "to that beacon light on high, to heaven's luminary, the source of light, and fountain of true wisdom—to the Throne of Grace…. His unswerving integrity, unyielding fidelity, and past experience fit" him for the crisis the country faced. Christian concluded by stating his faith that the war would soon be won and the whole land "renovated, regenerated and free from the black brittish stain of human slavery! America will then stand Redeemed." When that happy day comes, "The dutiful surviving soldier will return then from the toil and carnage to his peaceful home and loved ones and receive his well earned Reward. For right is right since God is God. And right the day must win; To doubt would be disloyalty. To falter would be sin."

Christian undoubtedly felt better after completing the lengthy, passionate letter. Obviously, Christian considered himself a true American patriot, and he forcefully articulated the belief that political support and patriotism would carry the country to victory. It was also apparent that he found nearly as much fault in the Copperhead element as he did in the Confederacy itself. This letter was a ringing endorsement for Lincoln's reelection and was probably submitted to a few newspapers for publication.[204]

A few days after his lengthy campaign message, Christian penned another letter containing some bad news. A wagon train coming from Fort Scott was "captured by the rebels between that place and Ft. Gibson." Although it was uncertain how many men were lost, Christian hopefully added that it was "presumed that nearly all got away unharmed." Significantly, this was the returning refugee train that Christian had tried hard to join. He wrote, "Here is a lesson for me and may also do for you, which tells me to humble myself before my merciful God, and be ever thankful for His guidance." The wagon train was attacked by Confederate general Stand Watie in support of General Sterling Price's Missouri expedition. Watie, in command of the Cherokee Brigade, was an effective and feared raider. The mention of his name in western Arkansas evoked terror, and he was often associated in both manner and effectiveness, "rightly or wrongly," with the name of William Quantrill. The Confederate Indians, in the Second Battle of Cabin Creek, captured about 130 wagons carrying $1.5 million in goods destined for sixteen thousand Unionist Indians. Christian did have some good news to report, as well. An interdenominational "Army Church" was holding meetings on Wednesday and Sunday. "We unite as one body from all denominations, taking the teachings of Jesus as the article of faith—you ought to have seen the eagerness of some to press forward to give in their names—of course I gave mine too." On another positive note, word was again going around camp that Christian's regiment would soon return to Kansas.[205]

Henry penned a letter for Elise on October 16 from Deep Bottom, near the Confederate capital. Henry had participated in another major battle and lost another good friend. John Dellenbach, from the Winesburg area, fell "in a way that it would make the boldest soldier shudder." Still, the regiment "pushed onwards that day yet to the very Gates of Richmond, our regt. being hardly 2½ miles from the city, as we had not troops enough to hold the position, we had to fall back again some distance and fortify a position, working day and night." After a few days, the rebels attacked with a "heavy force, but were repulsed with heavy slaughter." The Union forces then spent several days preparing to launch an assault against the well-fortified enemy line. The men were repulsed, at a high cost, and many were "slaughtered for nothing at all, as the result could plainly be foreseen—When we came within a few rods of the works we were received by a perfect hail of bullets, that raked our ranks terrible," and only an immediate retreat saved the men "from an entire annihilation." Henry compared the tremendous fire "to that terrible Ft. Wagner charge." Yet he was still "in the land of the living." Henry reported, "How soon we will have another struggle God only knows, but this is hardly the last we have to take part in before this summer campaign closes. Be my fate whatever, the Lord's will be done."[206]

Christian wrote to Elise from Horse Creek, Choctaw Nation, en route north. "We are getting along pretty well, but very slow. We average only about 12 miles a day. It took me 6 days to go from Ft. Smith to Ft. Gibson." As they neared the Cabin Creek battleground, Christian described a grisly scene. "One buried man was dug up by the wolves and the flesh eaten off." The refugee train that Christian was escorting was in desperate need of supplies and food, and they came upon some provisions from the ill-fated supply train that were guarded by loyal Indians. Christian wrote, "Let me assure you that those hard tacks brightened many a face & cheered many a heart. We had been without any bread for 2 days & in the Refugee camps was much suffering at Ft. Smith." Supplies were also low at Fort Gibson, and had they not been able to get provisions at Cabin Creek, "starvation would [have] unavoidably raged among us" before they reached Fort Scott. Christian, though, was worried about possible attacks on the rest of their journey. "The refugees were a disparate group of rich & poor, young & old, men, women & children." They had all kinds of transportation, and

Christian described it as the "most peculiar outfit I ever seen." The rich refugees, or at least those who were wealthy before the war, looked poor, and the less fortunate suffered from "intense poverty. Many children are without shoes, and but thinly clad in rags, many are sick and several died already, they are not only houseless & homeless, but also friendless & helpless, and most of them had once comfortable homes...but for their country's sake they became as poor paupers."[207]

Elise wrote a letter from Winesburg on October 23. She experienced some anxiety because of rumored rebel plunderers in Missouri, but neither she nor Christian provided further details. She anxiously awaited a letter from Christian stating that he was homeward bound. With winter approaching, she felt gloomy; it was hard to imagine spending another winter in Ohio. And yet, "the sorer my trials, the nearer am I to God." She avoided discussing politics or the election campaign "because I would not know where to begin." Finally, she again remarked that Christian's father was quite ill and spent most of his time in bed, which was of great concern to the family.[208]

On October 24, Christian wrote from Fort Scott, Kansas. Upon their arrival, Christian found the people in the highest state of excitement; the Rebels were reported to be advancing on the fort, and General Blunt had sent a dispatch ordering that all the commissary and ordnance should be moved away, as well as all the women and children. An attack was "expected hourly," and rumors were rampant in the climate of uncertainty. Christian, for example, reported the possibility that guerrillas were in the area. He made no mention in this letter of General Sterling Price, however, although the previous day, Price's large force had been defeated by Union troops at the Battle of Westport, near Kansas City.[209]

Christian recounted recent events in a letter dated October 26. After the Westport engagement, Price marched south toward Fort Scott. About 150 men of the 2nd Kansas went north to harass him. Christian was not among them, due to an illness diagnosed "by the Doctor who is in charge of us Invalids" and a "poor Pony." The doctor gave Christian permission to report to him at Fort Leavenworth no later than November 10. Christian hoped that he would then be discharged at Leavenworth because his term of enlistment was completed. He looked back with relief, "grateful to God that I am relieved from the scenes of carnage—not because I am no longer willing to do my duty, but as I am actually unable to undergo hardships as I did, we have reasons to rejoice that I am once more on Free Kansas soil." Under the circumstances, Christian anticipated no more direct contact with the enemy; any news he received of military activity would come secondhand.[210]

A letter written on October 30 from the Merwin House in Lawrence related that Christian had witnessed "a high state of excitement." Christian probably misdated his previous letter, as on Tuesday, October 25, Price and an army of 25,000 to 30,000 men marched by Fort Lincoln and came within five miles of Fort Scott. Only about 1,500 troops were at Fort Scott, including "militia, stragglers, & volunteer soldiers." But to the good fortune of Christian and the others, Price had been soundly beaten during the preceding days in several engagements, including the Battle of Mine Creek about twenty miles north of Fort Scott. In anticipation of Price's approach, the men of Fort Scott prepared themselves behind "breastworks or parapets." Christian was determined that "if the rebels do come I intend to give them the best I have." But Price's army was in complete retreat, and near Fort Scott, it "turned east" as Union troops continued their pursuit. Fort Scott then became the scene of celebration, as "the town was filled with troops and a fine Brass band...played the Beautiful National Air: The Star Spangled Banner. The strains nearly effected me to tears & filled my heart with thankfullness to God Almighty." On Thursday, Christian left Fort Scott and made his way toward Leavenworth, pausing at Prairie City and taking "dinner in the same House where dear departed Adolph died." At Lawrence, he decided to stay for several days and rest, having "had the chills every other day last week."[211]

Christian reported to Elise on November 2 that he arrived safely in Leavenworth and was staying at a friend's house. Christian was told that he would be mustered out in the next few days but cautioned Elise not to celebrate until she received the official word. He added, "Our joy has come in three doses." Christian had escaped the "scenes of carnage; and he would soon be mustered out. The third reason for joy was the hope of reunion," or as Christian wrote, "OUR MEETING." Only four days later, Christian wrote another letter from the home of Elise's father, Benjamin Dubach. Willow Dale held special meaning to Christian. During their courtship, he and Elise spent many joyful hours there, and he was reunited with family members for the first time in two years. Christian wrote that Elise's father and a young boy, probably a stepbrother to Elise, "were the first I have seen." As Christian approached, the two were out "in the cornfield cleaning beans. I got within a few steps of Father before he saw me, he was so rejoiced he did not know hardly what do to. He put his arms around me and wept—and thanked God for my return." Christian remarked that his joy was tempered by a "sad loneliness after you my Dearest." He might also have been reflecting on the death of his son; Elise had requested that Christian visit the baby's grave.

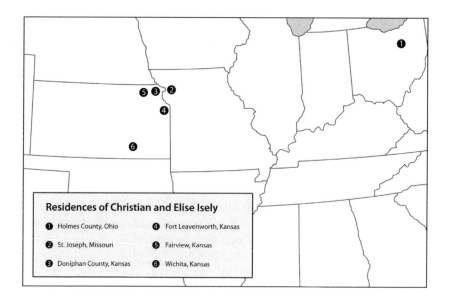

Residences of Christian and Elise Isely. *Map by Matt Walker.*

As Christian looked back on all that had transpired since his enlistment, he felt unworthy of the many blessings that God had bestowed on him. Elise's relatives told Christian that he looked "very bad, poor & lean." Christian, though, reported that he was "well again & have good appetite, and had no fever since last Sunday."[212]

On November 11, Christian wrote to Elise that he had returned to Leavenworth and learned the results of the presidential election. "There is great rejoicing," Christian exulted, "especially among the soldiers, over the reported results of the late Election, that honest old Abe is again elected by a large majority." Christian added that the returns indicated that Missouri went entirely Union, and "the State will now ere long be free from the CURSE, SLAVERY." Fort Leavenworth had undergone significant changes since Christian was there in April 1863, including the construction of two large hospital buildings and additional barracks. Five days later, Christian wrote the words that Elise longed to hear. "I have the Happiness to inform my cherrish One that I am now mustered out of the UNITED STATES SERVICE. I got my papers yesterday. Today I expect to be paid off." Christian and Elise's unshakeable faith had served them well, and Christian shared with Elise that God "spared me for you and you for me, may we only appreciate His goodness truely, and render unto Him the praise due as well as undivided

Love and Service." Christian rejoiced that he had survived three years of service without serious harm or injury to "either body or soul." His only injury was the loss of one tooth, which occurred after a scout. When he "returned to camp very hungry, finding nothing to satisfy my appetite, but a cracker box, I made a 'desperate charge,' siezed one of Uncle Sam's Pies [hardtack] and set my mastecaters at work, and Whack! Away went a tooth." Christian ended by imploring Elise to "give my love and high regard to All. And especially keep a Whole-Sale Abundance for Your Own Loving and Ever Devoted Husband, C.H. Isely."[213]

After a brief visit to St. Joseph, Christian headed for his boyhood home in Ohio. Elise remembered that when he arrived, he was "so yellow from malaria and so emaciated from starvation rations that I wondered how he could walk. He was very weak, but good food restored his health." In a short time, Elise wrote, "he was visiting his boyhood friends and wandering about his childhood haunts." On one particular visit to Winesburg, Christian entered a store owned by a member of the Joss family. Gottlieb and Martha Joss had shared their home in Leavenworth with Elise when Christian was first stationed there, and many of the Josses in Ohio were loyal Union supporters. When Christian entered the store, some of the men present criticizing the government were "friends of his youth and others to whom he had looked up when he was a mere child but who were now old men." This group of "Copperheads venomously denounced Grant" and predicted that "Lee would annihilate him." These words so angered Christian "that he could not keep his silence." Elise wrote that he vehemently "denounce[d] the assembly, charging those present with being traitors to their Fatherland, that, one after another, they hastily departed, except Colonel Joss." Joss, who generally remained silent in hopes of keeping his business, then spoke up. "'You gave it to them exactly right' he declared. 'They have been needing a talk like that for four years.'" Elise added that the event had a positive effect on Christian, and he came home elated. He had waged verbal warfare on Copperheads through the letters he wrote to Elise, and at Joss's store he took the opportunity to denounce some publicly.[214]

The war was over for Christian, but not for his brother Henry. The 67th Ohio was still in the eye of the storm, near Richmond in the winter of 1864–65. Henry received a letter from Christian stating that he had arrived in Ohio. Henry thankfully replied on December 16, looking forward to a reunion. "Though you and I may differ grossly in political matters, I hardly think that the happiness when we dare meet and welcome each other once more from face to face, would not be limited, after a seperation of more than

6 years." The last three years had been especially difficult because both men had spent their time "in the army, on the field of carnage, indeed nothing could be more welcome than such a meeting after the turmoil of war, right after returning from the bloody battlefields." On March 26, 1865, Henry wrote that a general movement of the army was soon to be made "before Richmond and Petersburg, and it is generally believed that the day is not far distant when we shall at last succeed to plant the Stars and Stripes upon the ramparts of Richmond."[215]

Henry's prediction of Union victory was on the mark. On the day of Lee's surrender, April 9, Union and Confederate forces skirmished near Appomattox Court House. Although Henry had been involved in many heated battles, it was on that day that an enemy bullet finally found him. About sunrise, Lee opened his final attack, on Union cavalry, and the 67th Ohio double-quicked two miles and arrived just in time to save the command of General Philip Sheridan from rout or capture. Henry's unit was part of the battle line, and "a shell from a rebel battery, about three hundred yards distant struck and splintered his gun and exploded within five feet of him, one fragment passing over, grazed his head and another cut to the skullbone." The force of the impact rendered Henry "insensible, but [upon] recovering," he found his way to the surgeon's quarters and was "ordered to be shipped back with the wounded. He refused, and rejoined his command in time to hear, the galloping couriers announce, 'Lee has surrendered.'"[216]

The assassination of President Abraham Lincoln within a week of Lee's surrender at Appomattox tempered the Union victory. This was a horrible blow to an already battle-scarred nation. Elise wrote later of the effect the news had on Christian, who admired Lincoln greatly. "I recall vividly how news came of the death of Lincoln. A day or two after the assassination, a neighbor…brought the word. I remember how we were shocked, especially Christian, who went to bed for three days." Elise wrote that even "the Copperheads were sorry." Suddenly, those who had despised him "had nothing but praise for the man whom they had criticized during the years of war."[217]

Henry recovered from his wounds, was mustered out of the service at Richmond on October 14, 1865, and returned home to his family in Ohio. In letters written shortly before his return, he instructed Christian to shelve the political differences around the family hearth. Judging by the volume of letters that exist, it is doubtful that Christian ever stopped discussing issues he deemed important. Nonetheless, the brothers shared a soldierly bond that surely endeared them to each other for the rest of their lives. Of the two brothers, Henry witnessed a great deal more combat, but both endured hardships. Christian campaigned on the western frontier, where supplies and rations were always scarce. It was often difficult to ascertain friend from foe, and the border warfare was especially brutal. Christian, especially in 1863 and 1864, was involved primarily with escort and scout duty. He never knew whether bushwhacker or thief lay hidden within the next grove of trees. He engaged the enemy in face-to-face combat about five times, although he often guarded or transported desperate men. According to family sources, Christian stated in later years that he never knowingly killed anyone. His letters and diaries reveal, however, that he witnessed the deaths of many and comforted some of his grievously wounded comrades as they departed the mortal for the eternal.[218]

Christian Isely, circa 1890s. *Courtesy the Isely family.*

Henry experienced a different type of warfare in the Eastern Theater. During the Battle of Weir Bottom Church on June 16, 1864, Henry "became

Elise Isely, circa 1890s. *Courtesy the Isely family.*

disconnected from his company and was attacked by three rebels, two of whom fired at him, but missed." Henry calmly loaded his gun and "brought one rebel down while the others fled." Henry had enlisted with five others from the Winesburg area in Company C of the 67th Ohio. "Companions in peace and comrades in war," they fought in "the same series of battles, until one by one they fell into patriots graves." Three were killed in combat, and one died in a Confederate prison and another of typhoid fever. Henry was the "only remaining one of the six brave boys who fought side by side in many bloody battles."[219]

Both Christian and Henry left friends and comrades in marked and unmarked graves on the field of battle. The memories of those encounters remained with them the rest of their lives. The events of their years of military service defined their entire lives. As Christian wrote, all those who participated in the conflict left their mark, whether good or bad. Christian wanted his legacy to be one of service to his God and country. He wanted his descendants to view him as one who willingly sacrificed everything he had for the country he loved—his adopted but much loved "sorely bleeding land." For Christian, Elise and Henry, the choices they made during the Civil War crafted a history of pride for them and for generations to come. For those three Swiss immigrants, who avoided shot, shell and the verbal barrages of their enemies, the war was over, the Union was preserved and they had survived.

EPILOGUE

As 1865 came to a close, Christian and Elise ended their stay in Ohio. Christian's father, Christian Isely II, had died the previous August. Initially, Christian and Elise returned to St. Joseph, where Christian resumed his trade as a carpenter. The church that they attended before the war survived, but the membership had changed substantially. Following the Civil War, things throughout the country would never be quite the same, and St. Joseph was no exception.

In 1872, Christian and Elise acquired some land in Brown County, Kansas, near the town of Fairview and relocated their growing family. A short time later, Henry, recently married to Sophia B. Hochstetler, also migrated to Brown County, as did Fred and his wife, Pauline Geiger Isely. They brought with them their aged mother, Barbara Ozenberger Isely. Christian soon set about building homes for his two brothers, as well as for other area residents. It was not an easy life. The Iselys battled drought and grasshoppers and faced many other difficulties.

Fred Isely spent the rest of his life in Brown County, Kansas. Sadly, he lost his only son in 1867 at the age of six. Fred and his wife, Pauline, were prosperous and active in the community around Fairview, Kansas, like his siblings. Fred served in some local offices, including on the school board and city council and as township treasurer. As Christian predicted, Fred, a lifelong Democrat, came to regret the choices he had made during the Civil War. The *Annals of Brown County, Kansas* notes that Fred was drafted in October 1862 and that while he reported to Camp Mansfield, he chose to pay

for a substitute to take a place. According to the *Annals*, Fred's decision to buy a substitute was based on his need to take care of the family homestead and his aged parents. That may be at least partially true, but certainly personal politics played a role in his decision— "This inability to defend his country has ever since caused him much regret." Clearly, living many years around Civil War veterans and of course around his two brothers, who were celebrated at Grand Army of the Republic (GAR) gatherings, was a painful reminder of the decisions and arguments that Fred had postulated during the war.[220]

Henry Isely and his wife, Sophia, also prospered on their Brown County farm. In addition to raising a family, Henry served as a teacher in the Fairview district school. In the mid-1870s, Henry was elected as the county clerk and later served on the Hiawatha City Council. His political experience finally led him to the Kansas House of Representatives. Although a

Top: Elise Isely, circa 1900. *Courtesy the Isely family.*

Left: Christian Isely, circa 1900. *Courtesy the Isely family.*

Henry Isely, circa 1890. *Courtesy Kansas State Historical Society.*

Democrat, he appealed to Republicans and Independents and later became a member of the growing People's Party in Kansas. His war record and leadership abilities made him the logical choice to be the leader of local GAR posts, and he served as the commander of the Sabetha Post. The *Annals* recorded, "He feels that the boys in blue are a little nearer and dearer than any other class of men and has demonstrated on many occasions his loyalty to his old comrades."[221]

Christian and Elise had eight sons and three daughters, eight of whom survived to adulthood. Their first children following the war were twins,

Fred and Pauline Isely, circa 1890. *Courtesy Kansas State Historical Society.*

Christian and Elise Isely in the woods, circa 1890s. *Courtesy the Isely family.*

William Henry and Mary Alice, born in August 1865. Christian and Elise encouraged all of their children to be well educated, and they succeeded admirably. William Henry Isely, after attending Harvard, served as a dean at Fairmount College, later known as Wichita State University. He encouraged his aging parents to come to Wichita as well. William Henry died suddenly in 1907 at the age of 42. Mary Alice led a colorful life. She was best known as a teacher and a librarian at Fairmount College. She died in 1969 at the age of 104. Many of Christian and Elise's other children were prominent in their respective fields. Bliss Isely, who helped his mother write her autobiography, *Sunbonnet Days*, was an accomplished historian and writer. Charles Christian Isely was a journalist and businessman and, in 1932, a candidate for the U.S. Senate. Others served as teachers, professors and missionaries. The list of accomplishments by

Christian Isely walking down road, circa 1900. *Courtesy the Isely family.*

Christian Isely mowing the lawn, Wichita, Kansas, circa 1915. *Courtesy the Isely family.*

Isely descendants could continue, but it is obvious that these children and grandchildren received unique training and support.

The family of Christian and Elise Dubach Isely on their fiftieth wedding anniversary, Wichita, Kansas, May 1911. *Courtesy Special Collections and University Archives, Wichita State University Libraries.*

Elise Isely with her great-grandchildren, Wichita, Kansas, circa 1935. *Courtesy the Isely family.*

Christian and Elise relocated to Wichita in 1907. They were certainly saddened in 1909 when they received news from Fairview that Henry had passed away. Christian was involved in the Grand Army of the Republic, Garfield Post No. 25, as well as with church functions. Christian died in Wichita in 1919 at the age of ninety-one. Elise remained involved in the church and continued to be an avid reader until her eyesight gave out in 1922. In 1935, she recounted to Bliss her fascinating life story, which became *Sunbonnet Days*. From crossing an unkind ocean at twelve to living on the eve of the Second World War at ninety, Elise had witnessed many changes. Although every family member of her generation was gone, and though blind, she asserted, "I enjoy this life and have many friends here...but on the other side are many waiting, who I will gladly join when the summons comes." The summons came for Elise the following year, in 1936, at the age of ninety-four.[222]

THE FAMILY OF CHRISTIAN AND ELISE DUBACH ISELY

Christian H. Isely (1828–1919)
Elise Dubach Isely (1842–1936)

Married on May 31, 1861, in St. Joseph, Buchanan County, Missouri.

CHILDREN:
Adolph Isely
William Henry Isely
Mary Alice Isely
John Calhoun Isely
Lydia Jeanette Isely
Olivia Grace Isely
Frederick Benjamin Isely
Charles Christian Isely
James Walter Isely
Bliss Isely
Dwight Isely

NOTES

CHAPTER 1

1. Christian H. and Elise Dubach Isely homepage.
2. Isely, *Sunbonnet Days*, 19–20. During the Civil War, in all the letters and communication, Elise's name is spelled "Eliza." The name was pronounced with an "s" sound, and according to family, Elise preferred the spelling with the "s" that was used in later years. Other than in direct statements made in letters, she will be referred to as "Elise" through the remainder of the work.
3. Ibid., 16–50.
4. Ibid.
5. Ibid., 51–61.
6. Ibid.

CHAPTER 2

7. Ibid., 61–63.
8. Johannsen, *Stephen A. Douglas*, 404.
9. Nevins, *Ordeal of the Union*, vol. 2, 92–93; Castel, *William Clarke Quantrill*, 1; Thayer, *History of the Kansas Crusade*, 31–32.
10. Abraham Lincoln to Joshua F. Speed, August 24, 1855, in Lincoln, *Life and Writings*, 395.
11. Rawley, *Race and Politics*, 81.

12. Goodrich, *War to the Knife*, 117–18.

13. Ibid., 128–29.

14. *Congressional Globe*, 34th Cong., 1st sess., Appendix: 536–37.

15. Donald, *Charles Sumner*, 293–300; Pierce, *Memoir and Letters*, vol. 3, 469–76.

16. Brown, *Reminiscences of Gov. R.J. Walker*, 73–74.

17. Nichols, *Bleeding Kansas*, 113.

18. Abels, *Man on Fire*, 83–87.

19. E.V. Sumner to Colonel S. Cooper, July 7, 1856, House, Executive Documents, Washington, D.C., 56–58; *Journal of the House of Representatives of Kansas* in Stephenson, *Political Career*, 67, n51; Etcheson, *Bleeding Kansas*, 115–18.

20. Gleed, "Samuel Walker," 271; Goodrich, *War to the Knife*, 151–54.

21. Villard, *John Brown*, 245–46, 248; Oates, *To Purge This Land*, 168–71.

22. Miner, *Kansas*, 78–80.

Chapter 3

23. Isely, *Sunbonnet Days*, 64–65, 77–78.

24. Ibid., 81, 101–2.

25. Ibid., 105–7.

26. Christian H. Isely (hereafter CHI) to Elise Dubach (hereafter ED until she and Christian marry), December 3, 1858, Isely Family Papers, ms 88-31, Box 1, FF 5. For the sake of continuity, unless otherwise mentioned, spelling and grammar from original letters or diary entries are unchanged.

27. CHI to ED, April 29, 1859, Isely Family Papers, FF 6.

28. ED to CHI, March 19, 1860, Isely Family Papers, FF 10.

29. Christian Iseley's Account Book of St. Joseph, Buchanan County, Missouri, from September 3, 1853, to June 4, 1860, private collection.

30. ED to CHI, July 1, 1860, Isely Family Papers, Box 1, FF 12; and CHI to ED, August 6, 1860, Isely Family Papers, FF 15.

31. Isely, *Sunbonnet Days*, 112.

32. Ibid., 112–14; CHI to EDI, May 31, 1861, Isely Family Papers, Box 1, FF 18.

33. Isely, *Sunbonnet Days*, 114.

34. Carr, *Missouri*, 267; Isely, *Sunbonnet Days*, 114–15.

35. Ibid., 115–16.

36. Logan, *Old Saint Jo*, 95–96.

37. Ibid., 96–97, 100.

38. CHI to Christian and Barbara Ozenberger Isely, October 19, 1856, Isely Family Correspondence and Miscellaneous Documents, Box 2, personal correspondence.

39. CHI to Abraham Lincoln, May 6, 1861, Isely Family Papers, Box 1, FF 16.

40. Ibid.

41. Isely, *Sunbonnet Days*, 114.

42. John Kunsly to CHI, June 23, 1861, Isely Family Papers, Box 1, FF 19. Note that the spelling of Kunsly's name changed throughout the course of his correspondence with Christian. Toward the later period, he wrote "Kunzli." He was also referred to as "Kunzli" by Elise and other Ohio relatives. Consequently, he will be referred to as "Kunzli" in the remainder of the text except in direct quotes.

Chapter 4

43. Castel, *General Sterling Price*, 3, 7, 50.

44. Isely, *Sunbonnet Days*, 119–22; Logan, *Old Saint Jo*, 104–5.

45. Ibid.

46. *Sunbonnet Days*, 121–22; Christian Iseley's Account Book, September 10, 1861.

47. CHI to mother, Barbara Ozenberger Isely, and sister, Annie B., September 17, 1861, Isely Family Papers, Box 1, FF 22.

48. Henry Isely (hereafter HI) to CHI, September 17, 1861, Isely Family Papers, FF 21.

49. Isely and Isely, *Uncommon Writings*, October 6–16, 1861.

50. Ibid., October 17–29, 1861.

51. Isely, *Sunbonnet Days*, 123–24; Elise Dubach Isely (hereafter EDI) to CHI, October 23, 1861, Isely Family Papers, Box 1, FF 23.

52. Roberts, *Encyclopedia of Historic Forts*, 296–97. The sketch made by Christian Isely of Fort Lincoln could refer to either Fort Lincoln near Fort Scott or Camp Lincoln near Fort Leavenworth. His comment on the sketch—"Sketched by Chr. H. Isely on the 9th day of May. Because he was attached to this Military Post more than the other ones"—would suggest that he is referring to the location closest to Fort Leavenworth. He was familiar with both locations, however, and the two were commonly referred to as Camp Lincoln (near Leavenworth) and Fort Lincoln (near Fort Scott).

53. CHI to EDI, November 10, 1861, Isely Family Papers, Box 1, FF 24.

54. Isely, *Sunbonnet Days*, 125–27.

55. Isely and Isely, *Uncommon Writings*, November 30–December 8, 1861.

56. John F. Ozenberger to "Cousin Isely" (CHI), November 18, 1861, Isely Family Papers, Box 1, FF 25.

57. CHI to EDI, November 21, 1861, Isely Family Papers, FF 27; Speer, *Life of General James H. Lane*, 252–64; Miner, "Lane and Lincoln," 186–99;

Cornish, *Sable Arm*, 69–70; United States War Department, *Official Records*, series 3, vol. 1, 280–81.

58. Isely and Isely, *Uncommon Writings*; CHI to his parents, Christian and Barbara Isely, in Winesburg, Ohio, December 15, 1861. This letter was written in German and was translated by Professor Jacob Heible, with the aid/transcription of David McGuire, Isely Family Papers, Box 1, FF 29.

59. George, *Sentinel of the Plains*, 119; Isely, *Sunbonnet Days*, 127–29.

60. Isely, *Sunbonnet Days*, 127–29.

61. Isely and Isely, *Uncommon Writings*, January 1, 1862.

62. Ibid., January 5, 7, 16–18, 28, 1862.

63. Ibid., January 20, February 4–5, 12, 1862.

64. Ibid., February 1, 7, 1862.

65. Ibid., February 20–22, 1862; Isely, *Sunbonnet Days*, 129–30.

66. CHI to EDI, February 24, 1862, Isely Family Papers, Box 2, FF 3.

67. Isely, *Sunbonnet Days*, 130–31.

68. Ibid., 129–30.

69. Isely and Isely, *Uncommon Writings*, February 24–March 3, 1862; Isely, *Sunbonnet Days*, 130–31.

70. Isely, *Sunbonnet Days*, 131; Isely and Isely, *Uncommon Writings*, March 3–26, 1862.

71. Isely and Isely, *Uncommon Writings*, April 11 and May 5, 9, 12, 16, 29–30, 1862; HI to CHI, May 20, 1862, Isely Family Papers, Box 2, FF 6.

72. CHI to John F. and Willie Ozenberger, May 29, 1862, Isely Family Papers, FF 7.

73. Isely and Isely, *Uncommon Writings*, June 26–30 and July 3–8, 1862.

74. Ibid., August 4–6, 1862.

CHAPTER 5

75. Isely and Isely, *Uncommon Writings*, August 22–27, 1862; EDI to CHI, August 23, 1862, Isely Family Papers, Box 2, FF 9.

76. CHI to EDI, September 2, 1862, Isely Family Papers, FF 11.

77. Ibid., FF 12.

78. Ibid., FF 13.

79. Ibid., FF 14; Goodrich, *Bloody Dawn*, 68–70; Leslie, *Devil Knows How to Ride*, 94–97.

80. CHI to EDI, Isely Family Papers, September 2, 1862, Box 2, FF 14.

81. John G. Fackler to CHI, September 11, 1862, Isely Family Papers, FF 15.

82. EDI to CHI, September 12, 1862, Isely Family Papers, FF 16; CHI to EDI, September 16, 1862, Isely Family Papers, FF 17; Leslie, *Devil Knows How to Ride*, 144–46.

83. EDI to CHI, September 19, 1862, Isely Family Papers, Box 2, FF 18.

84. CHI to EDI, September 24–25, 30, 1862, Isely Family Papers, FF 19–21.

85. EDI to CHI, October 5, 1862, Isely Family Papers, FF 22.

86. Isely and Isely, *Uncommon Writings*, October 6–8, 1862; CHI to EDI, October 9, 1862, Isely Family Papers, Box 2, FF 23.

87. EDI to CHI, October 17, 1862, Isely Family Papers, FF 25.

88. JGF to CHI, October 18, 1862, Isely Family Papers, FF 26.

89. Ibid., FF 28.

90. CHI to EDI, October 22, 1862, Isely Family Papers.

91. CHI to EDI, November 3–4, 9, 1862, Isely Family Papers, FF 31–32, 34.

CHAPTER 6

92. CHI to EDI, November 11, 1862, Isely Family Papers, Box 2, FF 35. The sister whom Christian refers to in his letter is Ann Barbara, or Barbara Ann Kendle. She and her husband, J.G. Kendle, are mentioned in several letters.

93. Isely and Isely, *Uncommon Writings*, December 3, 1862.

94. McPherson, *Battle Cry of Freedom*, 493–94.

95. HI to CHI, November 13, 1862, Isely Family Papers, Box 2, FF 37.

96. CHI to EDI, November 17, 1862, Isely Family Papers, FF 38.

97. EDI to CHI, November 30, 1862, Isely Family Papers, FF 42; CHI to EDI, December 2, 1862, Isely Family Papers, FF 43.

98. EDI to CHI, December 9, 1862, Isely Family Papers, FF 46–47.

99. EDI to CHI, December 25, 1862, Isely Family Papers, FF 48; Isely and Isely, *Uncommon Writings*, December 31, 1862.

100. Isely and Isely, *Uncommon Writings*, January 1, 1863; Isely, *Sunbonnet Days*, 133–34.

101. EDI to CHI, January 12, 1863, from a private collection; Isely, *Sunbonnet Days*, 132–33.

102. CHI to EDI, January 13, 1863, Isely Family Papers, Box 3, FF 2.

103. John Kunzli to CHI, January 14, 1863, Isely Family Papers, FF 5; CHI to EDI, January 13, 1863, Isely Family Papers, FF 3.

104. CHI to EDI, January 14, 1863, Isely Family Papers, FF 4; *Union Army*, vol. 8.

105. CHI to EDI, January 19, 1863, Isely Family Papers, Box 3, FF 7; EDI to CHI, January 23, 1863, Isely Family Papers, FF 8; EDI to CHI, January 27, 1863, Isely Family Papers, FF 9.

106. EDI to CHI, January 31, 1863, Isely Family Papers, FF 11.

107. Isely and Isely, *Uncommon Writings*, January 31, 1863.

108. CHI to EDI, February 9, 1863, Isely Family Papers, Box 3, FF 16.

109. CHI to EDI, February 18, 1863, Isely Family Papers, FF 17; CHI to EDI, February 24, 1863, Isely Family Papers, FF 20.

110. CHI to EDI, February 24, 1863, Isely Family Papers, FF 19.

111. CHI to EDI, March 3, 1863, Isely Family Papers, FF 22.

112. CHI to EDI, March 8, 1863, Isely Family Papers, FF 24; Isely and Isely, *Uncommon Writings*, March 12–17, 1863.

113. Isely and Isely, *Uncommon Writings*, March 18–19, 23–27, 1863.

114. HI to EDI, March 14, 1863, Isely Family Papers, Box 3, FF 24.

Chapter 7

115. EDI to CHI, March 28, 1863, Isely Family Papers, Box 3, FF 25; CHI to EDI, March 30, 1863, Isely Family Papers, Box 3, FF 27.

116. EDI to CHI, March 12, 1863, Isely Family Papers, FF 33; CHI to EDI, March 12, 1863, Isely Family Papers, FF 34.

117. Isely and Isely, *Uncommon Writings*, April 15–17, 1863; CHI to EDI, April 17, 1863, Isely Family Papers, FF 37. Note that the 3rd Wisconsin Cavalry patrolled the Kansas-Missouri border against bushwhackers during the Civil War. Orrin Britton survived the war, returned to Wisconsin and lived until 1923.

118. HI to CHI, April 22, 1863, Isely Family Papers, FF 39.

119. CHI to EDI, April 22, 1863, Isely Family Papers, FF 40; Roberts, *Historic Forts*, 297.

120. CHI to HI, May 7, 1863, Manuscript Collection, ms 139.03, Kansas State Historical Society.

121. Ibid., May 4, 1863; CHI to EDI, April 24, 1863, Isely Family Papers, Box 3, FF 42; CHI to EDI, April 26, 1863, Isely Family Papers, Box 3, FF 44; Cornish, *Sable Arm*, 69, 77–78.

122. CHI to EDI, April 24, 26, 1863, Isely Family Papers, FF 42; CHI to EDI, May 4, 1863, Isely Family Papers, FF 44.

123. EDI to CHI, May 2 and 3, 1863, Isely Family Papers, FF 46; CHI to EDI, May 12, 1863, Isely Family Papers, FF 49.

124. CHI to EDI, May 14, 1863, Isely Family Papers, FF 50; CHI to EDI, May 18, 1863, Isely Family Papers, FF 52. Note that Christian made no mention of the crime committed by the executed soldier.

125. CHI to EDI, May 18, 1863, Isely Family Papers.

126. CHI to EDI, May 25, 1863, Isely Family Papers, FF 55; EDI to CHI, May 25, 1863, Isely Family Papers, FF 56.

127. CHI to EDI, May 31, 1863, Isely Family Papers, FF 60; Fellman, *Inside War*, 165.

128. EDI to CHI, May 31, 1863, Isely Family Papers, Box 3, FF 59; EDI to CHI, June 7, 1863, Isely Family Papers, Box 4, FF 1.
129. CHI to EDI, June 8, 1863, Isely Family Papers, FF 2.
130. CHI to EDI, June 13, 1863, Isely Family Papers, FF 3.
131. CHI to EDI, June 13–14, 1863, Isely Family Papers, FF 4.
132. EDI to CHI, June 15, 1863, Isely Family Papers, FF 5.
133. CHI to EDI, June 21, 1863, Isely Family Papers, FF 8; CHI to EDI, July 1–2, 1863, Isely Family Papers, FF 12.
134. CHI to EDI, July 1–2, 1863, Isely Family Papers.

CHAPTER 8

135. Isely, *Sunbonnet Days*, 142; EDI to CHI, June 21, 1863, Isely Family Papers, Box 4, FF 6.
136. EDI to CHI, June 28, 1863, Isely Family Papers, FF 10. Scriptural reference to Matthew 10:16.
137. CHI to EDI, July 1–2, 1863, Isely Family Papers, FF 12.
138. Ibid.
139. CHI to EDI, July 1–2, 1863, Isely Family Papers, FF 12; CHI to EDI, July 3–5, 1863, Isely Family Papers, FF 13.
140. CHI to EDI, July 1–2 and 10, 1863, Isely Family Papers, FF 14.
141. EDI to CHI, July 16, 1863, Isely Family Papers, FF 15; EDI to CHI, August 2, 1863, Isely Family Papers, FF 18.
142. CHI to EDI, August 2–3, 1863, Isely Family Papers, FF 17.
143. CHI to EDI, August 3, 1863, Isely Family Papers, FF 19; CHI to EDI, August 8, 1863, Isely Family Papers, FF 20; Isely and Isely, *Uncommon Writings*, August 11, 1863.
144. CIII to EDI, August 2, 1863, Isely Family Papers, Box 4, FF 17; CHI to EDI, August 3, 1863, Isely Family Papers, Box 4, FF 19; EDI to CHI, August 23, 1863, Isely Family Papers, Box 4, FF 23.
145. CHI to EDI, August 3, 1863, Isely Family Papers, FF 19; CHI to EDI, August 8, 1863, Isely Family Papers, FF 20.
146. HI to CHI, September 2, 1863, Isely Family Papers, FF 26.
147. CHI to EDI, September 5, 1863, Isely Family Papers, FF 27.
148. *Report of the Adjutant General*, 32.
149. CHI to EDI, September 10, 1863, Isely Family Papers, Box 4, FF 30; Crawford, *Kansas in the Sixties*, 100–101.
150. Kennedy, *Civil War Battlefield Guide*, 221.
151. EDI to CHI, September 6, 1863, Isely Family Papers, Box 4, FF 28.
152. Castel, *Civil War Kansas*, 142–44; *Union Army*.

153. CHI to EDI, September 10, 1863, Isely Family Papers, Box 4, FF 30; Bearss and Gibson, *Fort Smith*, 271, 290; William F. Cloud to John McNeil, September 20, 1863, *Official Records*, 603.

154. CHI to EDI, September 10, 1863, Isely Family Papers, Box 4, FF 30; CHI to EDI, September 16, 1863, Isely Family Papers, Box 4, FF 31; Cloud to McNeil, September 20, 1863, *Official Records*, 603.

155. EDI to CHI, September 27, 1863, Isely Family Papers, Box 4, FF 35.

156. EDI to CHI, October 4, 1863, Isely Family Papers, FF 37.

CHAPTER 9

157. Kennedy, *Civil War Battlefield Guide*, 224.

158. CHI to EDI, October 12, 1863, Isely Family Papers, Box 4, FF 39.

159. HI to EDI, October 19, 1863, Isely Family Papers, FF 43.

160. EDI to CHI, October 18, 1863, Isely Family Papers, FF 42.

161. HI to CHI, November 3, 1863, in Isely and Isely, *Uncommon Writings*.

162. EDI to CHI, November 4, 1863, Isely Family Papers, Box 4, FF 52; EDI to CHI, November 6, 1863, Isely Family Papers, Box 4, FF 53. In her letter of November 6, Elise cited 1 John 4:20 in particular.

163. EDI to CHI, November 4, 1863, Isely Family Papers, Box 4, FF 52; EDI to CHI, November 6, 1863, Isely Family Papers, Box 4, FF 53.

164. CHI to EDI, November 6, 1863, Isely Family Papers, FF 54; Abel, *American Indian*, 308–12.

165. EDI to CHI, November 28, 1863, Isely Family Papers, FF 59.

166. CHI to EDI, November 29, 1863, Isely Family Papers.

167. CHI to EDI, December 5, 1863, Isely Family Papers, FF 62.

168. CHI to EDI, December 5 and 12, 1863, Isely Family Papers, FF 63.

169. CHI to EDI, December 19, 1863, Isely Family Papers, FF 65; CHI to EDI, December 25, 1863, Isely Family Papers, FF 67.

170. CHI to EDI, December 19 and 25, 1863, Isely Family Papers.

171. Isely and Isely, *Uncommon Writings*, December 31, 1863, and January 1, 1864.

172. John Kunzli to CHI, January 10, 1864, Isely Family Papers, Box 5, FF 2; Klement, *Limits of Dissent*, 1–2; HI to EDI, January 11, 1864, Isely Family Papers, Box 5, FF 3.

173. CHI to EDI, January 11, 1864, Isely Family Papers, Box 5, FF 4.

174. EDI to CHI, January 15, 1864 Isely Family Papers,, FF 5; EDI to CHI, January 23, 1864, Isely Family Papers, FF 9.

175. HI to CHI, January 18, 1864, Isely Family Papers, FF 6; CHI to EDI, January 31, 1864, Isely Family Papers, FF 10.

CHAPTER 10

176. EDI to CHI, February 4, 1864, Isely Family Papers, Box 5, FF 11.

177. Isely, *Sunbonnet Days*, 142–43.

178. EDI to CHI, February 14, 1864, Isely Family Papers, Box 5, FF 14.

179. CHI to EDI, February 7, 1864, Isely Family Papers, FF 12; CHI to EDI, February 14, 1864, Isely Family Papers, FF 14.

180. CHI to EDI, February 23, 1864, Isely Family Papers, FF 17; Isely and Isely, *Uncommon Writings*, February 21, 1864.

181. EDI to CHI, February 27, 1864, Isely Family Papers, Box 5, FF 18.

182. CHI to EDI, February 28, 1864, Isely Family Papers, FF 19.

183. CHI to EDI, March 1, 1864, Isely Family Papers, FF 20; CHI to EDI, March 8, 1864, Isely Family Papers, FF 22.

184. Ibid.

185. CHI to EDI, March 12, 1864, Isely Family Papers, FF 23; EDI to CHI, March 13, 1864, Isely Family Papers, FF 24.

186. EDI to CHI, March 25, 1864, Isely Family Papers, FF 26.

187. HI to CHI, March 26, 1864, Isely Family Papers, FF 27; EDI to CHI, April 1, 1864, Isely Family Papers, FF 28.

188. CHI to EDI, May 3, 1864, Isely Family Papers, FF 31; *Union Army*, vol. 8.

189. Kennedy, *Civil War Battlefield Guide*, 273–74; *Report of the Adjutant General*, 78–124; CHI to EDI, May 5, 1864, Isely Family Papers, Box 5, FF 32.

190. EDI to CHI, May 15, 1864, Isely Family Papers, FF 34.

191. CHI to EDI, May 18, 1864, Isely Family Papers, Box 5, FF 35; Kennedy, *Civil War Battlefield Guide*, 272–74.

192. CHI to EDI, May 18, 1864, Isely Family Papers, Box 5, FF 35; Isely, *Sunbonnet Days*, 150.

193. EDI to CHI, May 29, 1864, Isely Family Papers, Box 5, FF 37; EDI to CHI, June 6, 1864, Isely Family Papers, Box 5, FF 38.

194. CHI to EDI, June 10, 1864, Isely Family Papers, FF 39; Isely, *Sunbonnet Days*, 151–53.

195. HI to CHI, June 16, 1864, Isely Family Papers, Box 5, FF 41.

196. CHI to EDI, June 19, 1864, Isely Family Papers, FF 42; CHI to EDI, July 3, 1864, Isely Family Papers, FF 45.

197. CHI to EDI, July 8, 1864, Isely Family Papers, FF 46.

198. CHI to EDI, August 6, 1864, Isely Family Papers, FF 51.

199. CHI to EDI, August 18, 1864, Isely Family Papers, FF 56.

200. HI to CHI, August 19, 1864, Isely Family Papers, FF 57.

201. CHI to EDI, August 22, 1864, Isely Family Papers, FF 59.

202. CHI to EDI, August 27, 1864, Isely Family Papers, FF 60.
203. Ibid.

CHAPTER 11

204. CHI to EDI, September 24, 1864, Isely Family Papers, Box 5, FF 66.
205. CHI to EDI, September 26, 1864, Isely Family Papers, FF 68; Kennedy, *Civil War Battlefield Guide*, 218–19; Abel, *American Indian*, 329–32.
206. HI to CHI, October 16, 1864, Isely Family Papers, Box 5, FF 70.
207. CHI to EDI, October 19, 1864, Isely Family Papers, FF 71.
208. EDI to CHI, October 23, 1864, Isely Family Papers, FF 72.
209. CHI to EDI, October 24, 1864, Isely Family Papers.
210. CHI to EDI, October 26, 1864, Isely Family Papers, FF 74.
211. CHI to EDI, October 30, 1864, Isely Family Papers, FF 75.
212. CHI to EDI, November 2, 1864, Isely Family Papers, FF 76; CHI to EDI, November 6, 1864, Isely Family Papers, FF 78; EDI to CHI, November 10, 1864, Isely Family Papers, FF 80.
213. CHI to EDI, November 11, 1864, Isely Family Papers, FF 81; CHI to EDI, November 16, 1864, Isely Family Papers, FF 83.
214. Isely, *Sunbonnet Days*, 154–55.
215. HI to CHI, December 16, 1864, Isely Family Papers, Box 5, FF 85; HI to CHI, March 26, 1865, from a private collection.
216. *United States Biographical Dictionary, Kansas Volume*, 797–98.
217. Isely, *Sunbonnet Days*, 155.
218. Peggi Bell Johnson and David and Katherine Isely McGuire to Kenneth Spurgeon, January 3, 2000.
219. *United States Biographical Dictionary, Kansas Volume*, 797–98.

EPILOGUE

220. Harrington, *Annals of Brown County*, 544–45.
221. Ibid., 556–58.
222. Isely, *Sunbonnet Days*, 219.

BIBLIOGRAPHY

GOVERNMENT PUBLICATIONS

Congressional Globe, Containing the Debates and Proceedings, 1833–1873. 109 vols. Washington, D.C.: Blair and Rives, 1834–73.

Report of the Adjutant General of the State of Kansas, 1861–1865. Leavenworth, KS: Bulletin Cooperative Printing, 1867.

United States War Department. *The War of the Rebellion: A Compilation of the Official Records of the Union and Confederate Armies.* Series I, vol. 22, part 1, 1888. Washington, D.C.: Government Printing Office, 1881–1901.

PRIMARY SOURCES

Blunt, James G. "General Blunt's Account of His Civil War Experiences." *Kansas Historical Quarterly* 1 (1932): 211–65.

Christian H, and Elise Dubach Isely Homepage. Edited and compiled by John Mattox. "Of-By-For Ourselves, the Descendants of Christian and Elise Dubach Isely," unpublished, 1939. www.isely.info.

Crawford, Samuel. *Kansas in the Sixties.* Chicago: A.C. McClurg, 1911.

Douglas, Stephen A. *The Letters of Stephen A. Douglas.* Edited by Robert Johannsen. Urbana: University of Illinois Press, 1961.

Fisher, Hugh D., Reverend. *The Gun and the Gospel: Early Kansas and Chaplain Fisher.* New York: Medical Century Company, 1897.

Isely, Christian H. Letter to his brother, Henry Isely, May 4 and 7, 1863. MS 139.03, Manuscript Collection, Kansas State Historical Society.

Isely, Christian H., and Elise Dubach Isely. The Isely Family Papers (letters, papers and diaries donated by Katherine I. McGuire on behalf of the Isely family). MS 88-31. Wichita, KS: Wichita State University Special Collections.

———. *Uncommon Writings by Common Folk: The Isely Family Letters, Papers, and Diaries.* Edited by David and Kathleen McGuire. N.p.: self-published, 1988.

Isely, Elise Dubach, as told to Bliss Isely. *Sunbonnet Days.* Caldwell, ID: Caxton Printers, 1935.

Isely Family Correspondence and Miscellaneous Documents, 1849–1943, manuscript 7. Kansas Collection, Kenneth Spencer Research Library, University of Kansas.

Lincoln, Abraham. *The Life and Writings of Abraham Lincoln.* Edited by Philip Van Doren Stern. New York: Modern Library, 1999.

Pierce, Edward L., ed. *Memoir and Letters of Charles Sumner.* Vols. 1–4. Boston: Roberts Brothers, 1893.

Robinson, Charles. *The Kansas Conflict.* Lawrence, KS: Journal Publishing Company, 1898.

Thayer, Eli. *A History of the Kansas Crusade: Its Friends and Its Foes.* New York: Harper & Brothers, 1889.

SECONDARY SOURCES

Abel, Annie Heloise. *The American Indian in the Civil War, 1862–1865.* Lincoln: University of Nebraska Press, 1992.

Abels, Jules. *Man on Fire: John Brown and the Cause of Liberty.* New York: MacMillan Publishing Company, 1971.

Andreas, A.T. *History of the State of Kansas.* Chicago: A.T. Andreas Publishers, 1883.

Bailes, Kendell E. *Rider on the Wind: Jim Lane and Kansas.* Shawnee Mission, KS: Wagon Wheel Press, 1962.

Bearss, Ed, and Arrell M. Gibson. *Fort Smith: Little Gibraltar on the Arkansas.* Norman: University of Oklahoma Press, 1969.

Blackmar, Frank Wilson. *The Life of Charles Robinson.* Topeka, KS: Crane, 1902.

Breihan, Carl W. *Quantrill and His Civil War Guerillas.* Denver, CO: Sage, 1959.

Brewerton, G. Douglas. *The War in Kansas: A Rough Trip to the Border, Among New Homes and a Strange People.* New York: Derby and Jackson, 1856.

Britton, Wiley. *The Civil War on the Border.* 2 vols. New York: G.P. Putnam's Sons, 1891.

Brown, George W. *Reminiscences of Gov. R.J. Walker; With the True Story of the Rescue of Kansas from Slavery.* 2nd part. Rockford, IL: self-published, 1902.

Burns, C.R., ed. *The Commonwealth of Missouri: A Centennial Record*. St. Louis, MO: Bryan, Brand, 1877.

Carr, Lucien. *Missouri: A Bone of Contention*. Boston: Houghton Mifflin, 1888.

Castel, Albert. *Civil War Kansas: Reaping the Whirlwind*. Lawrence: University Press of Kansas, 1997. Originally published as a *Frontier State at War, 1861–1865*.

———. *General Sterling Price and the Civil War in the West*. Baton Rouge: Louisiana State University Press, 1968.

———. *William Clarke Quantrill: His Life and Times*. New York: Frederick Fell, 1962.

Connelley, William E. *Quantrill and the Border Wars*. New York: Pageant, 1956. Originally published in 1910.

Connelley, William E., ed. *History of Kansas*. 5 vols. Topeka: Kansas State Historical Society, 1928.

Cordley, Richard. *Pioneer Days in Kansas*. Boston: Pilgrim, 1903.

Cornish, Dudley Taylor. *The Sable Arm: Black Troops in the Union Army, 1861–1865*. Lawrence: University Press of Kansas, 1956.

Cutler, William G. *History of the State of Kansas, Brown County*. Part 21. Chicago: A.T. Andreas Publishers, 1883.

Donald, David. *Charles Sumner and the Coming of the Civil War*. New York: Alfred A. Knopf, 1960.

Eldridge, Shalor Winchell. *Recollections of Early Days in Kansas*. Topeka: Kansas State Historical Society, 1920.

Etcheson, Nicole. *Bleeding Kansas: Contested Liberty in the Civil War Era*. Lawrence: University Press of Kansas, 2004.

Faubion, Hazel A. *Tales of Old "St. Joe" and the Frontier Days*. St. Joseph: St. Joseph, Missouri Branch of the National League of American Pen Women, 1977.

Fellman, Michael. *Inside War: The Guerilla Conflict in Missouri During the American Civil War*. New York: Oxford University Press, 1989.

Fox, William F. *Regimental Losses in the American Civil War, 1861–1865*. 18th ed. Dayton, OH: Morningside House, 1985.

Frazer, Robert W. *Forts of the West*. Norman: University of Oklahoma Press, 1965.

Gaeddert, G. Raymond. *The Birth of Kansas*. Lawrence: University of Kansas Press, 1940.

Goetzmann, William H. *Army Explorations in the American West, 1803–1863*. New Haven, CT: Yale University Press, 1959.

Goodrich, Thomas. *Bloody Dawn: The Story of the Lawrence Massacre*. Kent, OH: Kent State University Press, 1991.

———. *War to the Knife: Bleeding Kansas, 1854–1861*. Mechanicsburg, PA: Stackpole, 1998.

Hale, Donald R. *We Rode with Quantrill: Quantrill and the Guerilla War as Told by the Men and Women Who Were with Him*. Lee's Summit, MO: Donald R. Hale, 1982.

Harrington, Grant W. ed., pub. *Annals of Brown County, Kansas from the Earliest Records to January 1, 1900*. Hiawatha, KS: Brown County, Kansas, 1903.

Hinton, Richard J. *Rebel Invasions of Missouri and Kansas and the Campaign of the Army of the Border Against General Sterling Price, in October and November, 1864*. Leavenworth, KS: T.W. Marshall, 1865.

Hovarth, Sue. *St. Joseph's Presbyterians, 1843–1993*. St. Joseph, MO: Presbyterians of St. Joseph, 1994.

Hunt, Elvid. *History of Fort Leavenworth, 1827–1927*. Fort Leavenworth, KS: General Service Schools Press, 1926.

Isely, Bliss, and W.M. Richards. *Four Centuries in Kansas*. Wichita, KS: McCormick-Mathers, 1936.

Johannsen, Robert W. *Stephen A. Douglas*. New York: Oxford University Press, 1973.

Kennedy, Francis H., ed. *The Civil War Battlefield Guide*. 2nd ed. Boston: Houghton Mifflin, 1998.

Klement, Frank L. *The Limits of Dissent: Clement L. Vanlandigham and the Civil War*. Lexington: University Press of Kentucky, 1970.

Klunder, Willard Carl. *Lewis Cass and the Politics of Moderation*. Kent, OH: Kent State University Press, 1996.

Leslie, Edward E. *The Devil Knows How to Ride: The True Story of William Clarke Quantrill and His Confederate Raiders*. New York: Da Capo, 1996.

Logan, Sheridan A. *Old Saint Jo: Gateway to the West, 1799–1932*. St. Joseph, MO: Platte Purchase Publishers, 1979.

McNeal, Thomas Allen. *When Kansas Was Young*. New York: MacMillan, 1922.

McPherson, James M. *Battle Cry of Freedom: The Civil War Era*. New York: Ballantine, 1989.

———. *Ordeal by Fire: The Civil War and Reconstruction*. New York: Alfred A. Knopf, 1982.

Miller, George. *Missouri's Memorable Decade, 1860–1870*. Columbia, MO: E.W. Stephens, 1898.

Miner, Craig. *Kansas: The History of the Sunflower State, 1854–2000*. Lawrence: University Press of Kansas, 2002.

———. "Lane and Lincoln: A Mysterious Connection." *Kansas History* (Autumn 2001): 186–99.

Monaghan, Jay. *Civil War on the Western Border*. Boston: Little, Brown, 1955.

Monnett, Howard N. *Action Before Westport, 1864*. Revised ed. Niwor: University Press of Colorado, 1995.

Moore, Miles. *Early History of Leavenworth City and County*. Leavenworth, KS: Samuel Dodsworth, 1906.

Morrison, Michael A. *Slavery and the American West: The Eclipse of Manifest Destiny and the Coming of the Civil War*. Chapel Hill: University of North Carolina Press, 1997.

Nevins, Allan. *Ordeal of the Union*. 2 vols. New York: Charles Scribner's Sons, 1947.

———. *The War for the Union*. 2 vols. New York: Charles Scribner's Sons, 1959.

Nichols, Alice. *Bleeding Kansas*. New York: Oxford University Press, 1954.

Oates, Stephen B. *The Approaching Fury: Voices of the Storm, 1820–1861*. New York: HarperCollins, 1997.

———. *To Purge This Land with Blood*: *A Biography of John Brown*. Amherst: University of Massachusetts Press, 1984.

Plummer, Mark A. *Frontier Governor: Samuel J. Crawford of Kansas*. Lawrence: University Press of Kansas, 1971.

Prentis, Noble L. *A History of Kansas*. Topeka, KS: Caroline Prentis, 1909.

Prucha, Francis Paul. *Army Life on the Western Frontier*. Norman: University of Oklahoma Press, 1958.

Rawley, James A. *Race and Politics—"Bleeding Kansas" and the Coming of the Civil War*. Philadelphia, PA: J.B. Lippincott, 1969.

Richmond, Robert W. *Kansas: A Land of Contrasts*. St. Charles, MO: Forum Press, 1974.

Roberts, Robert B. *Encyclopedia of Historic Forts: The Military, Pioneer, and Trading Posts of the United States*. New York: MacMillan, 1988.

Shindler, Henry. *Fort Leavenworth, Its Churches, and Schools*. Fort Leavenworth, KS: Army Service Schools Press, 1912.

Speer, John. *Life of General James H. Lane, Liberator of Kansas*. Garden City, KS: J. Speer, 1896.

Spring, Leverett Wilson. *Kansas: The Prelude to the War for the Union*. Boston: Houghton Mifflin, 1885.

Stephenson, Wendell Holmes. *The Political Career of General James H. Lane*. Topeka: Kansas State Historical Society, 1930.

Stratton, Joanna L. *Pioneer Women: Voices from the Kansas Frontier*. New York: Simon and Schuster, 1981.

Sullivan, Charles J. *Army Posts and Towns*. Los Angeles, CA: Burlington Free Press, 1926.

The Union Army: A History of Military Affairs in the Loyal States 1861–65; Records of the Regiments in the Union Army—Cyclopedia of Battles—Memoirs of Commanders and Soldiers. 8 vols. Madison, WI: Federal Publishing, 1908.

United States Biographical Dictionary, Kansas Volume, Containing Accurately Compiled Biographical Sketches, Into Which Is Woven the History of the State and Its Leading Interests. Kansas City, MO: S. Lewis, 1870.

Villard, Oswald Garrison. *John Brown, 1800–1859: A Biography Fifty Years After*. Boston, MA: Houghton Mifflin, 1910.

Walton, George. *Sentinel on the Plains: Fort Leavenworth and the American West*. Englewood Cliffs, NJ: Prentice-Hall, 1973.

Webb, Walter Prescott. *The Great Plains*. New York: Grosset and Dunlap, 1957.

Wilder, Daniel Webster. *The Annals of Kansas*. Topeka, KS: T.D. Thacher, 1886.

Williams, Robert H. *With the Border Ruffians—Memories of the Far West, 1852–1868*. Reprint. Lincoln: University of Nebraska Press, 1982.

JOURNALS AND MAGAZINES

Blackmar, F.W. "Charles Robinson." *Kansas Historical Collection* 6 (1897–1900): 187–202.

Blanton, B.F. "A True Story of the Border War." *Missouri Historical Review* (October 1922): 57–61.

Blunt, James G. "General Blunt's Account of His Civil War Experiences." *Kansas Historical Quarterly* 1 (1932): 211–65.

Caldwell, Martha B. "When Horace Greeley Visited Kansas in 1859." *Kansas Historical Quarterly* (1940): 115–40.

Gleed, Charles S. "Samuel Walker." *Kansas Historical Collections* 6 (1897–1900): 271.

Greene, Albert Robinson. "Campaigning in the Army of the Frontier." *Kansas Historical Collections* 14 (1915–18): 283–310.

Miner, Craig. "Lane and Lincoln: A Mysterious Connection." *Kansas History* 24 (2001): 186–99.

Tracy, Frank M., Col. "Capture of the Iatan Flag." *Kansas Historical Collections* 1–2 (1881).

NEWSPAPERS CONSULTED

Leavenworth Daily Conservative
Leavenworth Daily Times
St. Joseph Free Democrat
St. Joseph Weekly Free Democrat

INDEX

ABOUT THE AUTHOR

K en Spurgeon has spent the last fifteen years teaching at the middle, high school and college levels. He holds a BA and an MA in history from Wichita State University. He served for six years as the director of instruction for Cowley College, Arkansas City, Kansas. He currently is a history and government teacher at Northfield School of the Liberal Arts and at Newman University. Ken was the writer/producer of the Lone Chimney Films documentary *Touched by Fire: Bleeding Kansas, 1854–1861* and served as the writer/director for *Bloody Dawn: The Lawrence Massacre*. He was the cofounder of Lone Chimney Films Inc. and has served as the executive director since 2004. Ken and his wife, Amy, have four children and live on a farm near Towanda, Kansas.